Classroom-Ready

Number Talks

for Kindergarten, 1st and 2nd Grade Teachers

1000 Interactive Activities and Strategies That Teach Number Sense and Math Facts

Nancy Hughes

ULYSSES PRESS

Published in the United States by:
Ulysses Press
P.O. Box 3440
Berkeley, CA 94703
www.ulyssespress.com

ISBN: 978-1-61243-891-7
Library of Congress Control Number: 2018967971

Printed in the US by Kingery Printing Company, United Graphics Division
10 9 8 7 6 5 4

Acquisitions editor: Casie Vogel
Managing editor: Claire Chun
Editor: Shayna Keyles
Proofreader: Renee Rutledge
Front cover design: Justin Shirley
Cover art: kitten © Andrey1005/shutterstock.com; ball of string © Rvector/shutterstock.com
Interior design: Jake Flaherty
Interior art: See page 209

Contents

Grade 2 127

Introduction

History of Number Talks

Number talks were initially developed in the 1990s by Kathy Richardson and Ruth Parker in response to a professional development session for teachers. Although they have been around for some time, I didn't learn about number talks until 2010, when a sales representative gave me a complimentary copy of Sherry Parrish's *Number Talks: Helping Children Build Mental Math and Computational Strategies*. At the time, I was looking for a way to support mental math and computational strategies in the math classroom, and Parrish's book provided that needed support.

Much of my work with number talks, including this book, is based on earlier work of Richardson, Parker, and Parrish. Parrish's initial suggestions on setting up and executing an effective number talk can be easily implemented when working with students in any setting. This book's intent is to provide examples of number talks based on specific reasoning strategies aligned to Common Core math fluency standards. These reasoning strategies provide support for struggling learners by suggesting concrete and pictorial representations, as well as abstract mental computational strategies appropriate for the grade level.

Importance of Number Talks

There are many benefits to utilizing number talks on a daily basis. Number talks are a valuable classroom routine for developing efficient computational strategies, making sense of math, and communicating mathematical reasoning. A number talk is structured to help students conceptually understand math without memorizing a set of rules and procedures. Instead, they help students understand numerical relationships, such as composing (putting together existing numbers) and decomposing (breaking numbers into their subparts), using the base ten system, and learning properties of operations.

The primary goal for a number talk is to improve computational fluency (flexibility with computational methods, ability to explain and discuss a reasoning strategy, and computation with accuracy). Sharing math strategies during a number talk clarifies the student's thinking and helps develop the language of math. Students learn that numbers are made up of smaller numbers that can be composed and decomposed to make new numbers. They have the opportunity to think first and self-correct if needed.

Below are seven great components of a number talk, the first being most important. Number talks should help students:

+ Build computational fluency

+ Continue mental computation practice, which builds fluent retrieval of basic facts

+ Actively engage in learning

+ Focus on number sense and mathematical communication

+ Elicit efficient and accurate computational skills

+ Understand the relationships between numbers by modeling strategies

+ Move from concrete to representational to abstract thinking

If your goal is to improve computational skills, number talks are extremely useful, whether in the classroom, as an intervention, in homeschool settings, or for parents wanting to improve their child's math skills.

Format of a Number Talk

A daily number talk provides five to ten minutes for students to build fluent retrieval of basic arithmetic facts.

+ Select a math problem for the class

+ Provide wait time for all students to come up with an answer and a strategy

+ Students use mental math, not paper and pencil, to find a solution

+ Students give a thumbs-up when they have a solution or strategy

+ Randomly call on a few students to give their answers

+ Record student strategies and thinking for all to see

+ Ask several students to share their strategies

+ Students make corrections if needed

+ Students decide which answer is correct

+ If necessary, model explicit strategies and multiple examples

Conceptual Understanding Leads to Procedural Fluency

Math is a skill that must be developed over time, and it is essential that basic skills are practiced and reinforced daily. Number talks are a powerful way to enable students to become mathematical thinkers, efficient and accurate with computation, and ready to problem solve.

In order for students to be proficient in their mathematical thinking and reasoning, it is important that they have a strong understanding of number relationships. Number talks help students see the relationships between numbers by discussing and sharing various computational strategies. Teaching, reviewing, and reinforcing reasoning strategies gives students the tools they need for lifelong learning. Each student will comprehend math differently, so teaching multiple strategies in a variety of ways is necessary for all students to make sense of math.

The number one complaint from teachers is that struggling learners do not know their basic facts and cannot compute or reason with numbers. However, math is built on effort, not ability. Early math deficits have devastating effects on later learning. It is essential for students to understand computation so they will become procedurally fluent. Fluency involves knowing reasoning strategies and when to use them. Students must be not only flexible with numbers, but they must be efficient and accurate as well. For example, counting on fingers is a strategy, but it is not an efficient strategy.

To become fluent, it is essential to have the daily ongoing practice that number talks provide. It is important to move students from concrete to representational to abstract thinking. Number talks can move students from concept learning to understanding the relationships between numbers, then on to recalling facts quickly, efficiently, and accurately.

An important aspect of a number talk is that students articulate and share their strategies. Sharing strategies with other students through a number talk provides the means to explain, justify, and make sense of math.

On the next page you will see the required fluency standards by grade level. Keep these in mind as you use number talks in whole group, small group, or intervention settings. If students are struggling with a number talk, step back to easier numbers or introduce an easier strategy. If the computation is abstract, consider a representational model or if that is too difficult, use a concrete model.

REQUIRED FLUENCY ACCORDING TO COMMON CORE STATE STANDARDS

Kindergarten

K.OA.A.5 Fluently add and subtract within five.

K.OA.A.3 Decompose numbers less than or equal to 10 into pairs in more than one way, e.g., by using objects or drawings, and record each decomposition by a drawing or equation (e.g., 5 = 2 + 3 and 5 = 4 + 1).

K.OA.A.4 For any number from one to nine, find the number that makes 10 when added to the given number, e.g., by using objects or drawings, and record the answer with a drawing or equation.

K.NBT.A.1 Compose and decompose numbers from 11 to 19 into 10 ones and some further ones, e.g., by using objects or drawings, and record each composition or decomposition by a drawing or equation (such as 18 = 10 + 8); understand that these numbers are composed of 10 ones and 1, 2, 3, 4, 5, 6, 7, 8, or 9 ones.

First Grade

1.OA.B.3 Apply properties of operations as strategies to add and subtract.

1.OA.B.4 Understand subtraction as an unknown-addend problem.

1.OA.C.6 Add and subtract within 20, demonstrating fluency for addition and subtraction within 10.

1.OA.D.8 Determine the unknown whole number in an addition or subtraction equation relating three whole numbers.

1.NBT.C.4 Add within 100, including adding a two-digit number and a one-digit number, and adding a two-digit number and a multiple of 10, using concrete models or drawings and strategies based on place value, properties of operations, and/or the relationship between addition and subtraction; relate the strategy to a written method and explain the reasoning used. Understand that in adding two-digit numbers, one adds tens and tens, ones and ones; and sometimes it is necessary to compose a ten.

1.NBT.C.5 Given a two-digit number, mentally find 10 more or 10 less than the number, without having to count; explain the reasoning used.

1.NBT.C.6 Subtract multiples of 10 in the range 10–90 from multiples of 10 in the range 10 – 90 (positive or zero differences), using concrete models or drawings and strategies based on place value, properties of operations, and/or the relationship between addition and subtraction; relate the strategy to a written method and explain the reasoning used.

Second Grade

2.OA.A.1 Use addition and subtraction within 100 to solve one- and two-step word problems involving situations of adding to, taking from, putting together, taking apart, and comparing, with unknowns in all positions, e.g., by using drawings and equations with a symbol for the unknown number to represent the problem.

2.OA.B.2 Fluently add and subtract within 20 using mental strategies. By end of Grade 2, know from memory all sums of two one-digit numbers.

2.OA.C.3 Determine whether a group of objects (up to 20) has an odd or even number of members, e.g., by pairing objects or counting them by twos; write an equation to express an even number as a sum of two equal addends.

2.OA.C.4 Use addition to find the total number of objects arranged in rectangular arrays with up to five rows and up to five columns; write an equation to express the total as a sum of equal addends.

2.NBT.B.5 Fluently add and subtract within 100 using strategies based on place value, properties of operations, and/or the relationship between addition and subtraction.

2.NBT.B.6 Add up to four two-digit numbers using strategies based on place value and properties of operations.

2.NBT.B.7 Add and subtract within 1000, using concrete models or drawings and strategies based on place value, properties of operations, and/or the relationship between addition and subtraction; relate the strategy to a written method. Understand that in adding or subtracting three-digit numbers, one adds or subtracts hundreds and hundreds, tens and tens, ones and ones; and sometimes it is necessary to compose or decompose tens or hundreds.

2.NBT.B.8 Mentally add 10 or 100 to a given number 100–900, and mentally subtract 10 or 100 from a given number 100–900.

2.NBT.B.9 Explain why addition and subtraction strategies work, using place value and the properties of operations. (Explanations may be supported by drawings or objects.)

The Eight Common Core State Standards for Mathematical Practice

1. Make sense of problems and persevere in solving them.

2. Reason abstractly and quantitatively.

3. Construct viable arguments and critique the reasoning of others.

4. Model with mathematics.

5. Use appropriate tools strategically.

6. Attend to precision.

7. Look for and make use of structure.

8. Look for and express regularity in repeated reasoning.

Kindergarten

These number talks focus on the required fluency standards for each grade level, outlined on pages 5 to 6. For kindergarten, the proficiency standard asks students to be proficient with addition and subtraction within five.

K.OA.A.5 Fluently add and subtract within five.

K.OA.A.3 Decompose numbers less than or equal to 10 into pairs in more than one way, e.g., by using objects or drawings, and record each decomposition by a drawing or equation (e.g., 5 = 2 + 3 and 5 = 4 + 1).

K.OA.A.4 For any number from one to nine, find the number that makes 10 when added to the given number, e.g., by using objects or drawings, and record the answer with a drawing or equation.

K.NBT.A.1 Compose and decompose numbers from 11 to 19 into 10 ones and some further ones, e.g., by using objects or drawings, and record each composition or decomposition by a drawing or equation (such as 18 = 10 + 8); understand that these numbers are composed of 10 ones and 1, 2, 3, 4, 5, 6, 7, 8, or 9 ones.

In this section are the following addition strategy examples with suggested number talks:

Subitize

I see 3 circles.

I know because I see 2 circles and 1 more. 2 plus 1 is 3.

TIPS

- Provide sufficient wait time and allow all students the opportunity to answer and provide the strategy they used to get the answer.
- Subitizing helps students see number relationships and have number conversations. Being able to subitize is the cornerstone of mathematics.
- Students should be able to know how many dots there are without having to physically count each dot. Determining the number of dots should be done quickly at a glance.

QUESTIONS

- What do you see?
- How many circles/dots do you see?
- How did you come up with your answer?
- What number is one more?
- What number is one less?
- If I rearrange the objects, will I still have the same number?

Subitize: Number Talks

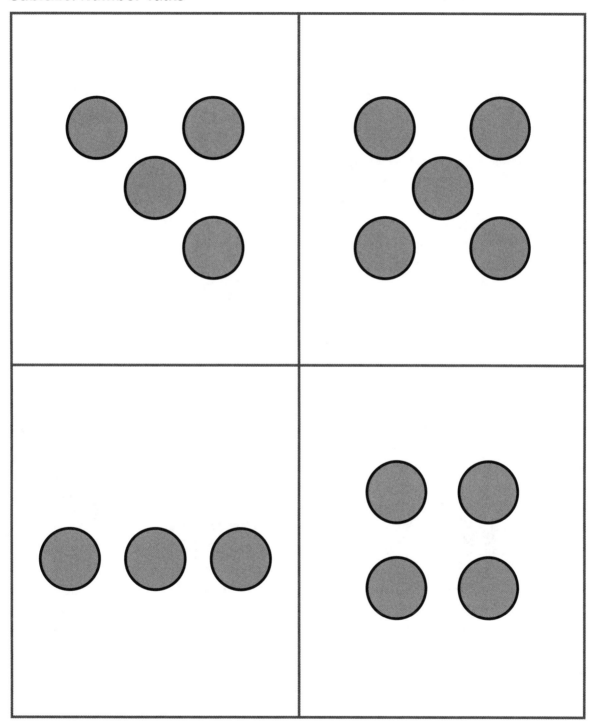

Subitize: Number Talks

Subitize: Number Talks

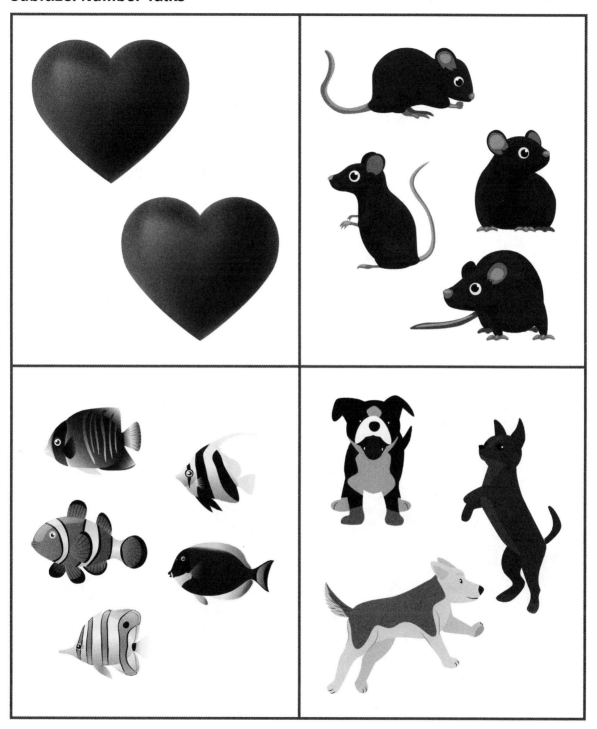

Subitize: Number Talks

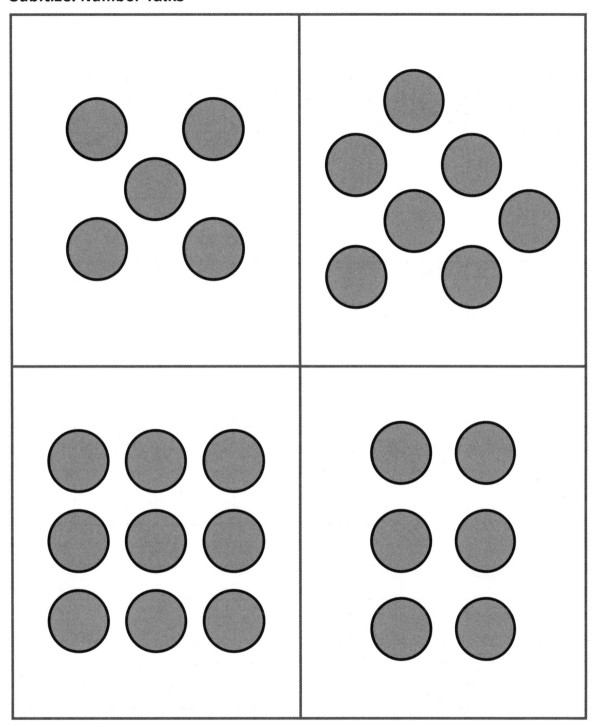

Subitize: Number Talks

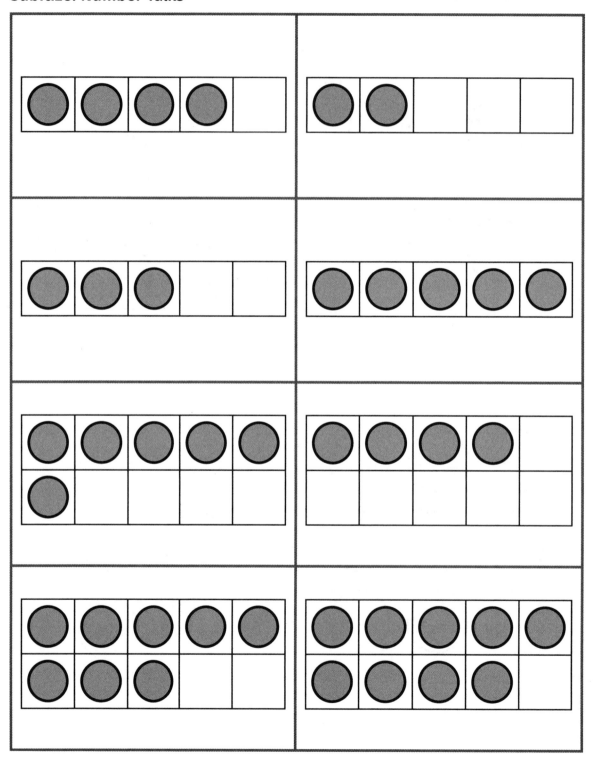

Subitize: Number Talks

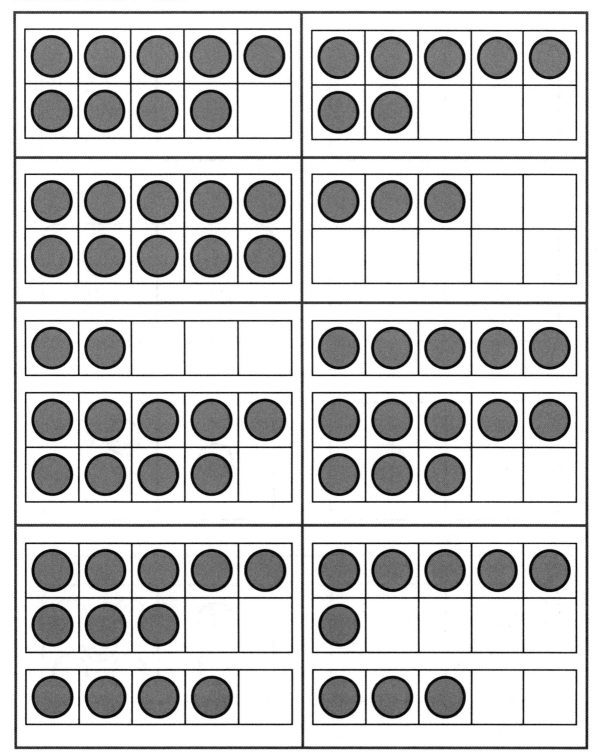

Subitize: Number Talks

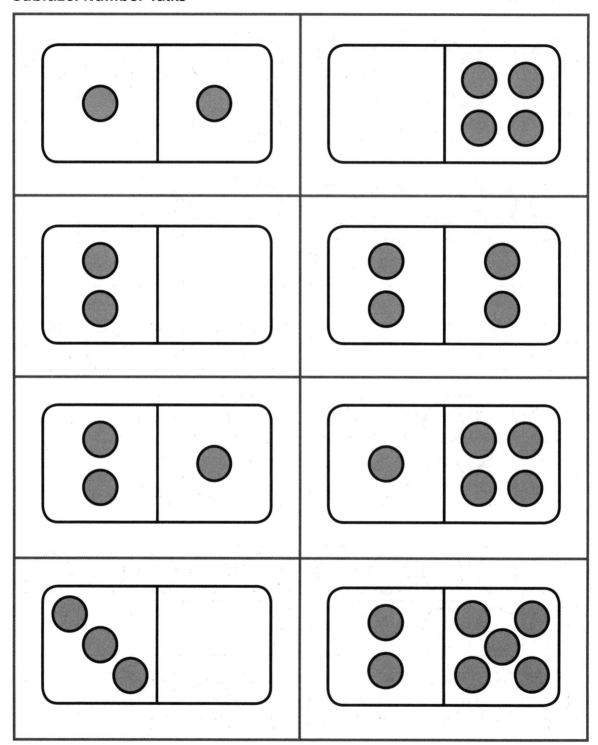

Subitize: Number Talks

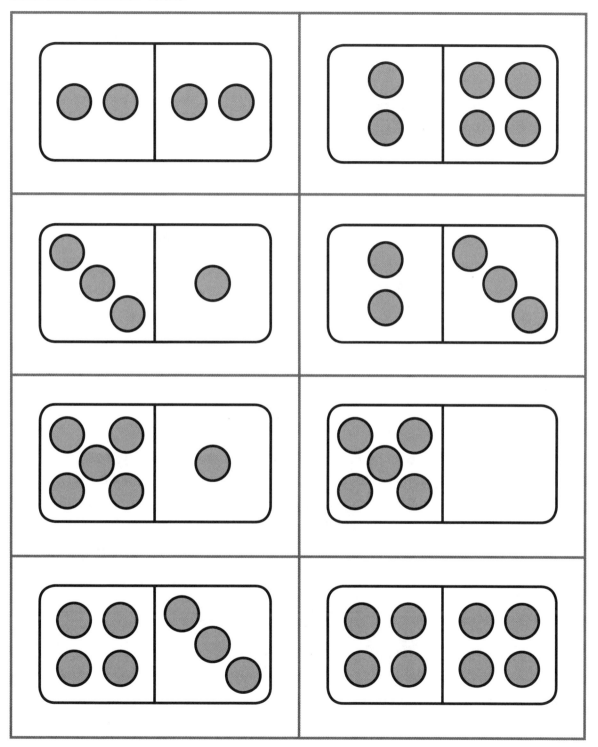

Number Bonds

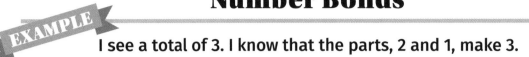
I see a total of 3. I know that the parts, 2 and 1, make 3.

My number sentence is 2 + 1 = 3.

I also know that 3 − 2 = 1 and 3 − 1 = 2.

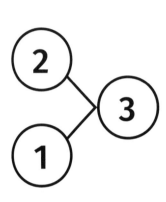

TIPS

- Number talks strengthen both conceptual understanding and procedural knowledge.
- Number bonds are used to help students see how numbers are combined (composed) or taken apart (decomposed).
- If a student is struggling with number bonds, use concrete models that will allow students to manipulate objects to make numbers and decompose numbers.
- Number bonds are ideal for helping students understand how numbers work by showing relationships between numbers.

QUESTIONS

- What do you see?
- Is a part of the number bond missing? What is the missing number?
- Can you come up with a number sentence to match the number bond?
- Identify the parts of the number bond.
- Identify the whole in the number bond.

Number Bonds: Number Talks

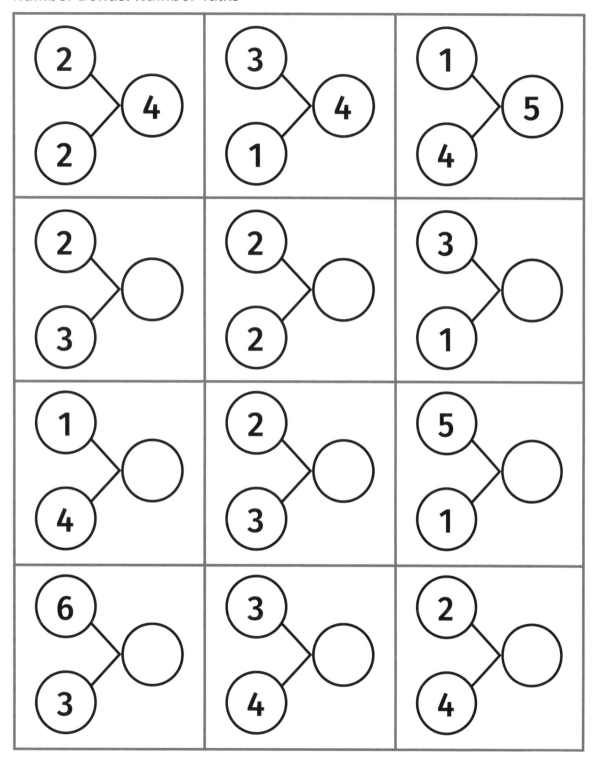

Number Bonds: Number Talks

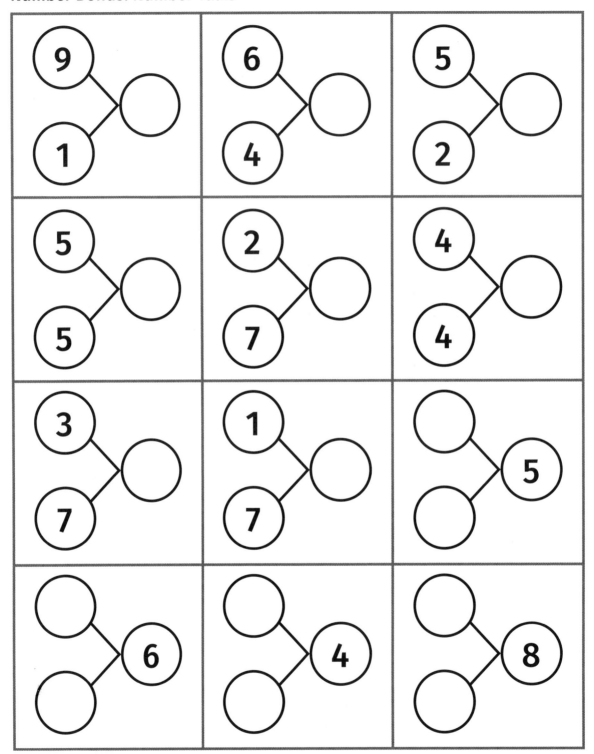

Number Bonds: Number Talks

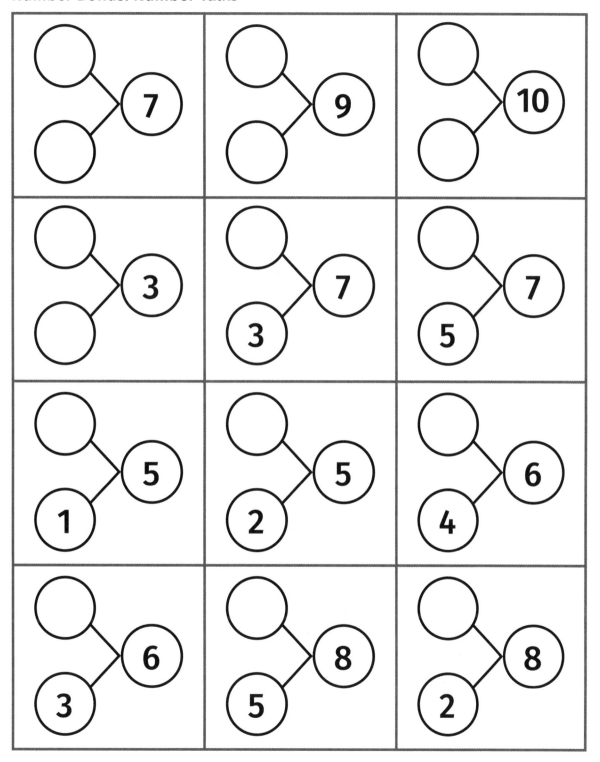

Number Stories

I see 2 dragons. 1 dragon crossed the bridge
and another is waiting to cross.

$1 + 1 = 2.$

TIPS

- Number talks help students verbalize their reasoning and explain their solutions. Keep mathematical practices in mind during a number talk.

- A number talk should be short and done daily. It should not take the place of core instruction.

- Have students tell you a counting story centered on the picture. Start by asking, "What do you see in this picture?" Welcome all responses from students.

QUESTIONS

- What do you see?
- Fill in a number bond based on this story.

- What number sentence can you make from this story?
- What if one of the dragons went away?
- What if one more dragon joined in?

Number Stories: Fish Tales

QUESTIONS

- What do you see?

- Can you tell me a counting story about what you see in the tank?

- How many fish do you see?

- If I took one fish out of the tank, how many would be left?

- Tell me a story using the number bond 2, 3, and 5.

- Tell me a story using the number bond 1, 4, and 5.

- How many fish have stripes? How many fish do not have stripes?

Number Stories: Pool Party

QUESTIONS

- What do you see?
- Can you tell me a counting story about what you see at the pool party?
- How many friends do you see?
- Tell me a story using the number bond 3, 4, and 7.
- Tell me a story using the number bond 2, 5, and 7.
- How many friends are girls? How many friends are boys? Are there more boys or girls?
- If 2 more friends came to swim, how many friends would there be for the pool party?

Number Stories: All Aboard

QUESTIONS

- What do you see?
- Can you tell me a counting story about what you see in the bus?
- How many riders do you see?
- Tell me a story using the number bond 1, 3, and 4.

- Tell me a story using the number bond 2, 2, and 4.
- If 1 more got on the bus, how many riders would there be? How did you solve this problem?
- Can you give me a number sentence that describes the picture?

Number Stories:
Ten-Frame

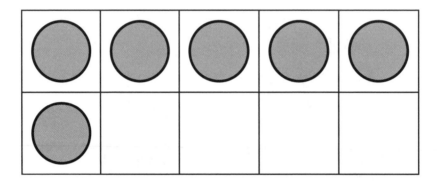

QUESTIONS

- What do you see?
- How many counters are on the ten-frame? How many more do you need to make 10?
- Can you give me a number sentence using the ten-frame?
- Can you show me a number bond using 3, 3, and 6?
- Can you show me a number bond using 6, 4, and 10?
- Can you show me a number bond using 5, 1, and 6?
- How did you find your answer? What strategy did you use?
- Did anyone use another strategy?
- Which strategy was easier for you?

Number Stories: Mountain Climbing

QUESTIONS

- What do you see?
- How many climbers are in this picture? What strategy did you use to find your answer?
- How many friends are climbing the mountain and how many are on the ground?
- How many dark caps do you see? How many pairs of shoes do you see?
- Are there more friends than shoes? How many more shoes do you see than friends?
- Can you tell me a number bond using 4, 5, and 9?
- Can you give me a number sentence using this picture?
- Can anyone give me a different number sentence using this picture?

Number Stories: Traveling by Train

QUESTIONS

- How many cars are on the tracks?

- How many animals are on the train?

- Can you tell me a story using a number bond with 4, 2, and 6?

- Can you give me a number sentence based on this picture?

- How many wheels do you see? What strategy did you use to find the number of wheels?

- If 2 more animals got on the train, how many would be on the train?

- If 4 animals got off the train, how many animals would be left on the train? How do you know?

Number Stories:
Apple Picking

QUESTIONS

- What do you see?
- How many apples are on the tree? How many apples are on the ground?
- How many fewer apples are on the ground than in the tree?
- How many more apples are in the tree than on the ground?
- How many total apples are there? What strategy did you use to find your answer?
- Did anyone else have a different strategy?
- If 3 apples fall off the tree, how many apples are left in the tree?
- Can you give me a number sentence that would describe the apples in this picture?

Number Stories:
Birding

QUESTIONS

- What do you see?

- How many birds are in the tree?

- How many birds are not in the tree?

- How many birds do you see in total?

- What strategy did you use to find the total number of birds? Can you explain your strategy?

- What number sentence can you use to describe the number of birds?

- If 2 more birds flew in, how many birds would be in the picture?

- If 4 birds flew away, how many birds would be left?

- Can you explain your thinking?

Number Stories: Butterfly Garden

QUESTIONS

- What do you see?
- How many butterflies do you see?
- How many butterflies have their wings closed for landing?
- How many butterflies have their wings open for flight?
- Can you tell me a story about this picture using a number sentence?

- What strategy did you use to find the total number of butterflies? Can you explain your thinking?
- Can you share your strategy with another classmate?
- Can you find a number sentence to describe your thinking? Does anyone have a different number sentence?

Number Stories: Road Construction

QUESTIONS

- What do you see?
- How many construction workers do you see?
- What strategy did you use to find your answer? Can you share your thinking?
- Did anyone use a different strategy? What strategy did you use?
- Can you give a number sentence to explain your answer?
- How many workers are on the ground and how many are on a machine?
- If 3 more workers arrive, how many workers will there be?
- Can you share your answer with your classmates? What strategy and thinking did you use?

Add To or Take From

2 owls are sitting on a log. 3 more join them.

I used the addition strategy of joining 2 and 3 together to get 5. I know that 2 jumps on the number line followed by 3 jumps will land me on the number 5. 2 + 3 = 5.

TIPS

- Number talks provide five to ten minutes for students to build fluent retrieval of basic arithmetic facts.
- Teach students to respect each other's discussion points during a number talk.
- Encourage conceptual explanations instead of procedural discussion. Celebrate thinking and understanding rather than answer getting.

QUESTIONS

- What do you see?
- Can you use jumps on a number line to show the answer?
- What number sentence can you use to find your answer?
- Does anyone have a different strategy?
- Can you use color counters to show this problem?

Add To or Take From: Number Talks

6 cups sat on the table. 2 fell off the table.
How many are on the table now?

5 animals are on the bus. 3 animals are waiting to get on the bus.
How many animals will be on the bus when the 3 waiting animals get on the bus?

4 bees are flying in the garden. 2 more join them.
How many bees are now in the garden?

Add To or Take From: Number Talks

Some bugs were in a jar. 2 more bugs were put in the jar.
Now there are 6 bugs in the jar.
How many were there to begin with?

5 pies were on the table. 4 pies are eaten at dinner.
How many pies are left?

4 children were seated at a table. Some of the children left.
Then there were 2 children. How many children left the table?

Add To or Take From: Number Talks

Carrie made 6 peanut butter and jelly sandwiches. She ate 2 for lunch.
How many sandwiches are left?

3 friends were picking apples.
Some more friends joined them.
Then there were 5 friends in total.
How many friends joined them?

4 people were going on vacation.
Then 1 decided to stay at home.
How many will now go on vacation?

Add To or Take From: Number Talks

Quinn is watching caterpillars. She sees 7 caterpillars. Then 2 walk away.
How many are left?

9 zebras are riding in a train. The train stops and 2 get off.
How many are left on the train?

5 children are flying kites.
2 children join them.
How many children are flying kites?

Making 5 or 10

I count 3 dots and 2 empty spaces.
I know that 3 and 2 make 5.

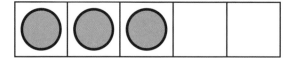

TIPS

- Number talks should be a daily classroom routine for making sense of mathematics.
- After one student shares a strategy, have another student repeat the strategy in their own words to anchor comprehension.
- For struggling students, use color tiles and a five-frame or ten-frame.
- It takes time for students to become proficient with number talks. Don't give up!

QUESTIONS

- What do you see?
- How many dots are there?
- How many empty spaces are there?
- How do you know you are right?
- What number sentence could you use for this five-frame?

Making 5 or 10: Number Talks

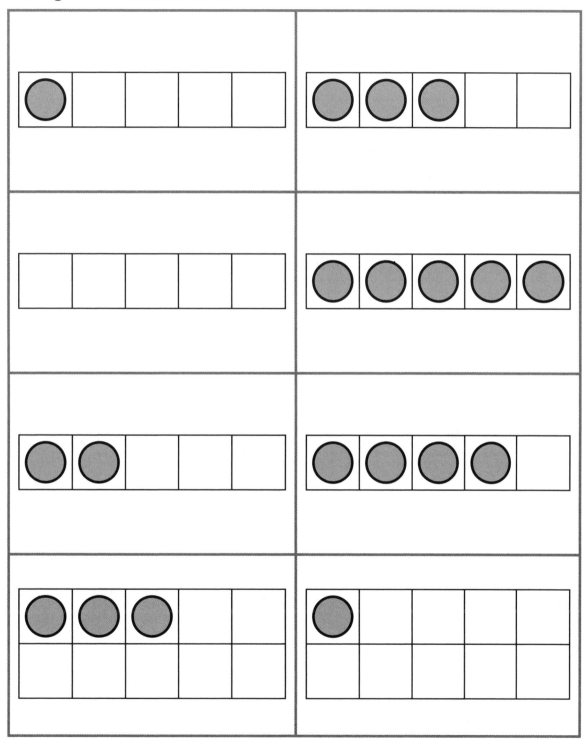

Making 5 or 10: Number Talks

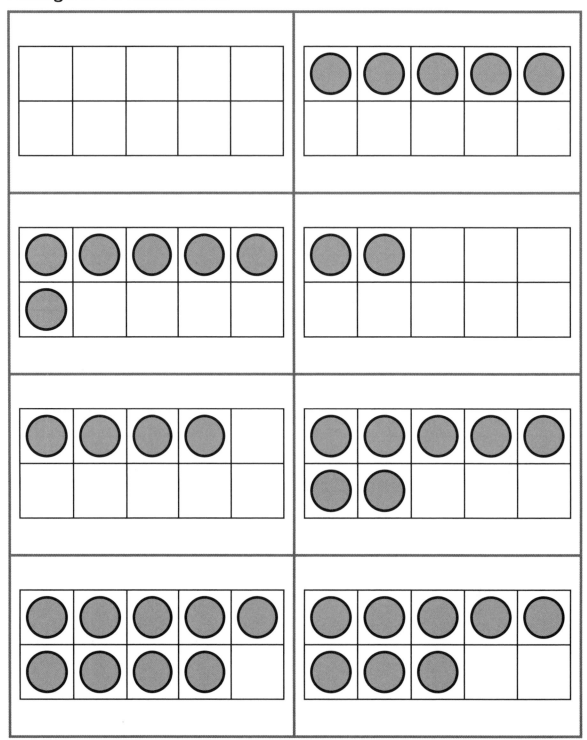

Writing an Equation

I see 2 black cars and 1 gray car on the train.
I know that 2 and 1 make 3. 2 + 1 = 3.

TIPS

- Number talks are ideal for developing efficient computational strategies.
- Allow a student to defend or disprove a strategy, just as long as it is done respectfully.
- Remember that the goal of a number talk is to teach computational fluency and conceptual understanding.
- Do not let students rely on procedures only.

QUESTIONS

- What do you see?
- How many black cars are there?
- How many cars are gray?
- Can you share a number sentence for this train?
- What number bond is the same as this picture?
- Can you share a number story using this picture?
- Three cars is the same as...?

Writing an Equation: Number Talks

Writing an Equation: Number Talks

Writing an Equation: Number Talks

Writing an Equation from a Number Line

I see one frog jumping from 0 to the number 4.

I see a second frog jumping 2 more places, from 4 to 6.

My number sentence is 4 + 2 = 6.

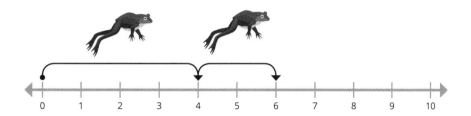

TIPS

- Number talks develop computational fluency.
- It is customary to use a thumbs-up approach to give students time to think about the problem and find a strategy for a solution.
- Use a number talk to help students discover their growth mindset.
- Provide support for students so they see multiple ways of solving a problem.

QUESTIONS

- What do you see?
- What equation or number sentence can you write based on the number line?
- What are the parts and what is the whole?
- Can you use a ten-frame to show this story problem?
- What is the answer to this equation? What strategy did you use?
- Can you explain your thinking?

Writing an Equation from a Number Line: Number Talks

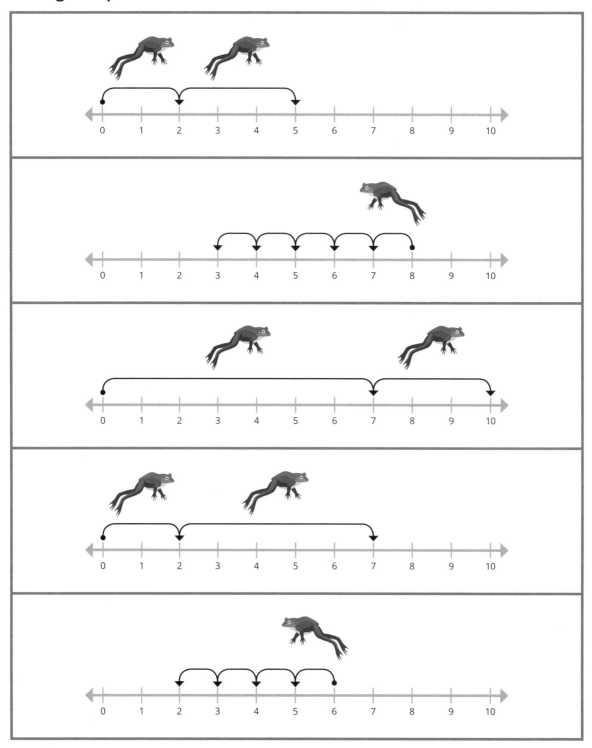

Writing an Equation from a Number Line: Number Talks

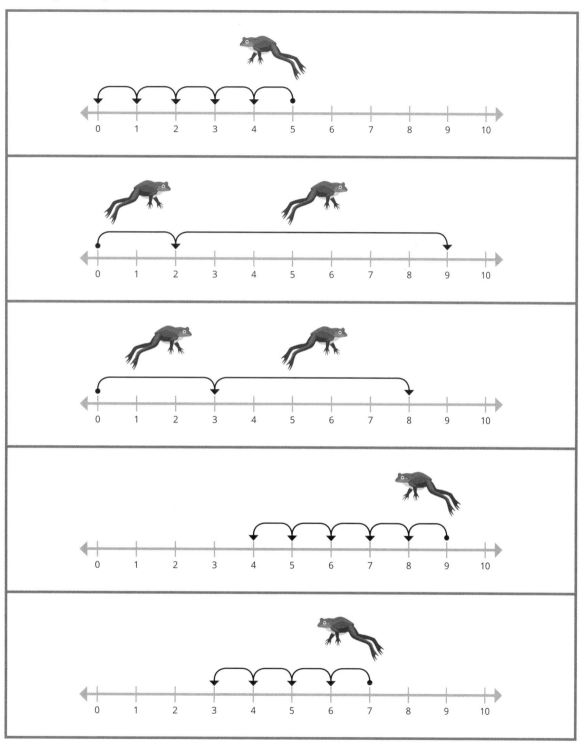

Writing an Addition Equation
from Ten-Frames

I see how 3 dark butterflies and 4 light butterflies make a
total of 7 butterflies. I know that 3 + 4 = 7.

TIPS

• A number talk should be short and done daily. It should not take the place of core instruction.

• The purpose of a number talk is to provide ongoing practice with mental computation.

• During a number talk, question students to delve deeper into their thinking processes.

• Number talks help students verbalize their reasoning and explain their solutions.

• Keep mathematical practices in mind during a number talk.

QUESTIONS

• What do you see?

• What strategy did you use to find your equation and answer?

• Can you explain your thinking?

• Can you show your thinking using color counters or a number line?

• What number sentence did you use?

Writing an Addition Equation from Ten-Frames: Number Talks

Writing an Equation from Ten-Frames: Number Talks

Writing an Equation from Ten-Frames: Number Talks

Writing an Equation from Ten-Frames: Number Talks

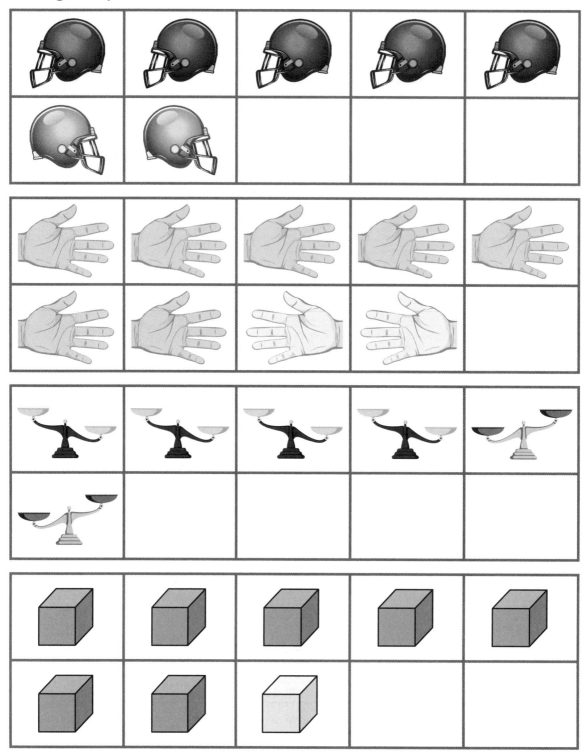

Writing an Addition Equation
Using Dominoes

EXAMPLE

I count 1 dot on the right and 2 dots on the left.
I know that 1 plus 2 is 3. 1 + 2 = 3.

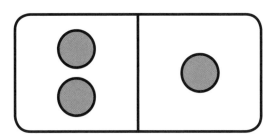

TIPS

- For struggling learners, use manipulatives such as color counters to find the total.
- Always start with small numbers and build up for success.
- Number talks help build fluid retrieval of basic math facts by modeling explicit strategies and using multiple examples.

QUESTIONS

- What do you see?
- How many dots are on the domino?
- What number sentence gives you the total number of dots?
- Can you describe your thinking?
- Can you think of a math story to go along with the domino?
- Would my total change if I add the 1 to the 2 or the 2 to the 1?

Writing an Addition Equation Using Dominoes: Number Talks

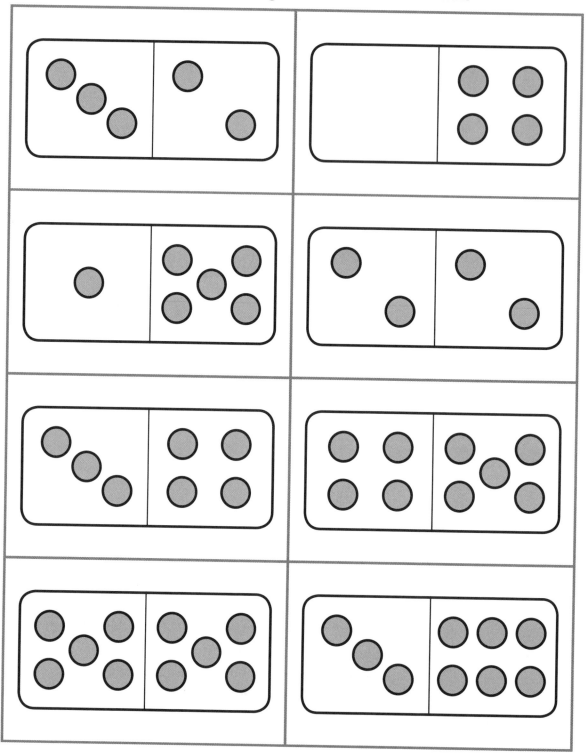

Writing an Addition Equation Using Dominoes: Number Talks

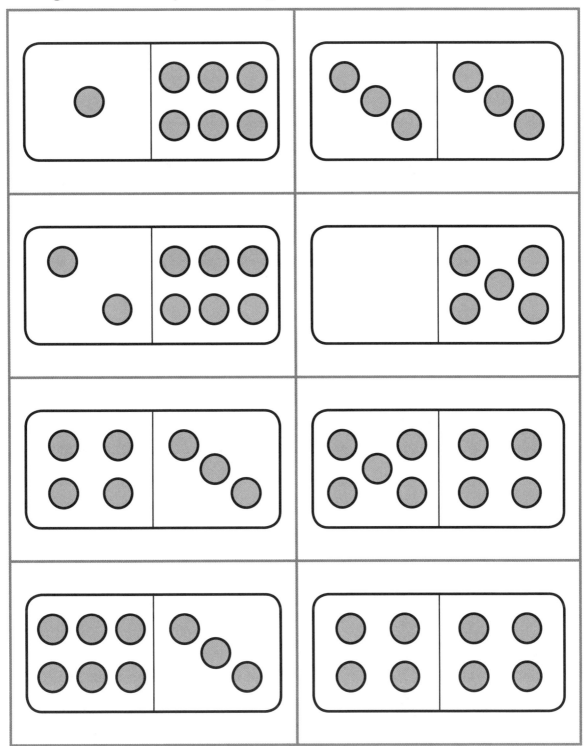

Writing a Subtraction Equation from Ten-Frames

I count 5 birds. Two of the 5 birds have been crossed out, leaving 3 birds. I know that 5 − 2 = 3.

TIPS

- A number talk will provide explicit instruction on prerequisite skills.
- Encourage curiosity and discovery during a number talk.
- Help students connect ideas, and explain the different representations of numbers.
- Explanations are classroom discussions which are critical for building mathematical understanding.

QUESTIONS

- What do you see?
- How many birds are there in total and how many were removed?
- How is this ten-frame different from addition ten-frames?
- If I remove 2 of the birds, how many do I have left?
- What number sentence can you use to describe the math?
- How can you prove your answer using a number line?
- What number bond describes this problem?

Writing a Subtraction Equation from Ten-Frames: Number Talks

Writing a Subtraction Equation from Ten-Frames: Number Talks

Writing a Subtraction Equation from Ten-Frames: Number Talks

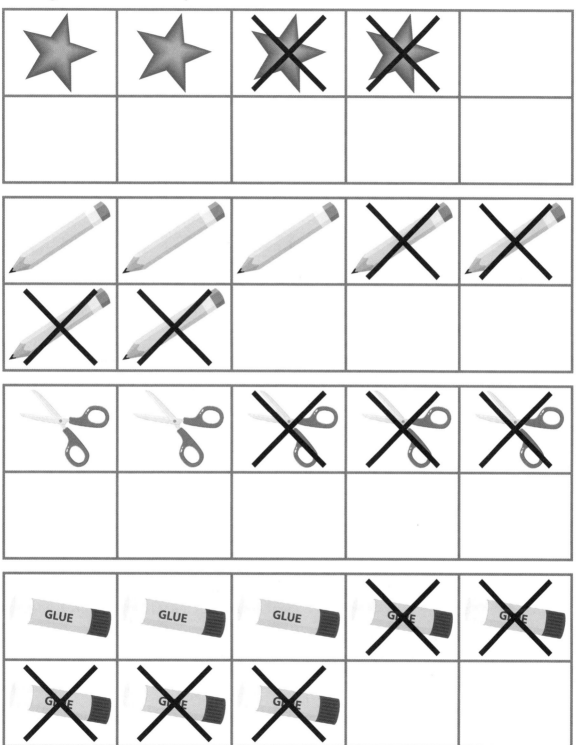

Part-Part-Whole

I see a whole of 5. Part of the whole is 3,
so the other part must be 2.
I know this because 3 + 2 is the same as 5.

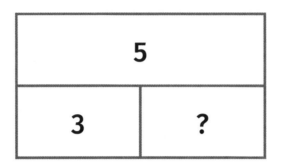

TIPS

- Number talks help communicate mathematical reasoning.
- A number talk is not a spiral review of math skills. It is meant as a tool for developing computational fluency through conceptual understanding.
- During a number talk, continue to ask questions to encourage rich discussions among students.

QUESTIONS

- What do you see?
- What number is the whole? What number is a part?
- What is the missing number?
- What strategy did you use to find the missing part?

- Can you tell me a number story using these 3 numbers?
- Can you give me an addition sentence based on these numbers?
- Can you give me a subtraction sentence using these three numbers?

Part-Part-Whole: Number Talks

5	
3	?

5	
4	?

?	
3	2

?	
4	1

6	
5	?

6	
3	?

6	
2	?

7	
?	4

7	
5	?

7	
?	1

Part-Part-Whole: Number Talks

8	
3	?

8	
?	2

8	
?	1

?	
5	3

?	
5	4

9	
?	3

10	
8	?

10	
?	4

10	
5	?

?	
7	3

Grade 1

These number talks are aligned with standards for first grade, with an emphasis on the standards requiring students to add and subtract within 20 with fluency within 10, as outlined on page 5. These number talks include standards supporting addition and subtraction within 10. The strategies described in this chapter are essential for developing conceptual understanding and procedural fluency: counting on, decomposing a number leading to 10, relationships between addition and subtraction, and equivalent or easier sums.

As you present a number talk, keep in mind the Eight Common Core State Standards for Mathematical Practice from page 7.

1.OA.B.3 Apply properties of operations as strategies to add and subtract.

1.OA.B.4 Understand subtraction as an unknown-addend problem.

1.OA.C.6 Add and subtract within 20, demonstrating fluency for addition and subtraction within 10.

1.OA.D.8 Determine the unknown whole number in an addition or subtraction equation relating three whole numbers.

1.NBT.C.4 Add within 100, including adding a two-digit number and a one-digit number, and adding a two-digit number and a multiple of 10, using concrete models or drawings and strategies based on place value, properties of operations, and/or the relationship between addition and subtraction; relate the strategy to a written method and explain the reasoning used. Understand that in adding two-digit numbers, one adds tens and tens, ones and ones; and sometimes it is necessary to compose a ten.

1.NBT.C.5 Given a two-digit number, mentally find 10 more or 10 less than the number, without having to count; explain the reasoning used.

1.NBT.C.6 Subtract multiples of 10 in the range 10 – 90 from multiples of 10 in the range 10 – 90 (positive or zero differences), using concrete models or drawings and strategies based on place value, properties of operations, and/or the relationship between addition and subtraction; relate the strategy to a written method and explain the reasoning used.

In this section are the following addition strategy examples with suggested number talks:

Add and Subtract Using Connecting Cubes

What is 6 + 2 = 8?

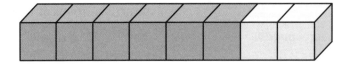

I have 6 connecting cubes. If I connect 2 more cubes, I will have a total of 8 cubes. I know that 6 cubes plus 2 more is 8 cubes. I also know that I can take the 8 connecting cubes and snap off 2 of the cubes to give me 6 cubes. 8 − 2 = 6.

TIPS

- You can use connecting cubes to introduce this addition strategy to students; this is a form of concrete representation.
- Record all responses (even incorrect answers) for students to see.
- Give struggling students the connecting cubes to add or subtract.
- Record student strategies. Ask students to turn to their neighbor and discuss and explain the strategy they used.

QUESTIONS

- How many cubes do you see? Use a thumbs-up when you have an answer.
- Can you explain the strategy you used?
- Did anyone use a different strategy?
- Can you give a number sentence to match the cubes shown?
- How many cubes were there before some cubes were removed or added?
- What is the correct answer? How do you know?

Add and Subtract Using Connecting Cubes: Number Talks

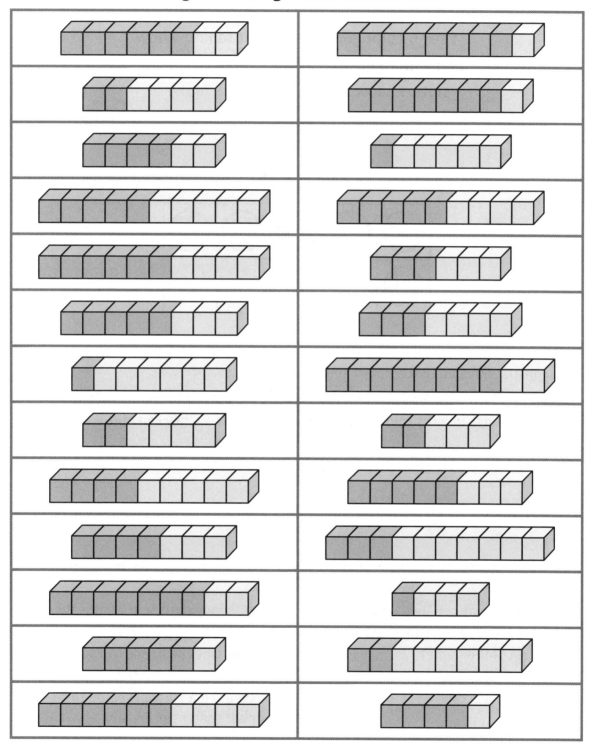

Make a 10

I see 6 color counters. I want to know how many more I need to make 10. I see 4 empty slots. I know that 6 and 4 more make 10.

$$6 + \_\_ = 10$$

$$6 + 4 = 10$$

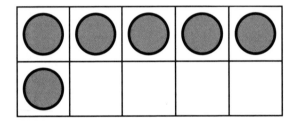

TIPS

- Demonstrate this problem using a single ten-frame.
- Help students write a number sentence that will completely fill in the frame.
- Give struggling students color counters and ten-frames so they can mirror the problem.
- Keep the mathematical practices in mind during a number talk.

QUESTIONS

- How many gray counters do you count?
- How many counters will it take to fill in the rest of the frame?
- How many total counters will fill the frame?
- What is my unknown?

- What are my parts and what is the whole?
- What number sentence can you use to fill in the frame?
- Can you tell a story based on the number sentence? Explain.

Make a 10: Number Talks

Addition with Regrouping on a Ten-Frame

What is 9 + 6?

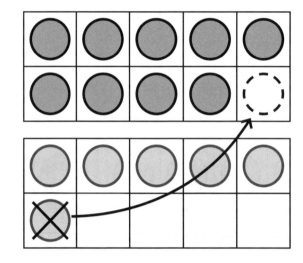

Answer

15

I see 1 ten-frame with 9 dark color counters and 1 with 6 light color counters. How many do I have altogether? I can move 1 light counter to join the 9 dark counters; now, I have 10 counters in the upper frame and 5 left over in the lower frame. 10 and 5 is the same as 15, which is easier to add. Thus, 10 + 5 = 15 and 9 + 6 is also 15.

TIPS

• Demonstrate this problem using 2 ten-frames and 15 color counters.
• Give struggling students the color counters and ten-frames so they can mirror the problem.

QUESTIONS

• How many total light counters and dark counters do you see? Use a thumbs-up when you have an answer.

• Can you explain the strategy you used to find the total?

• How does filling the top ten-frame make addition easier?

• Can you explain this strategy to a friend?

• Is there another strategy that works as well? Explain.

Addition with Regrouping on a Ten-Frame: Number Talks

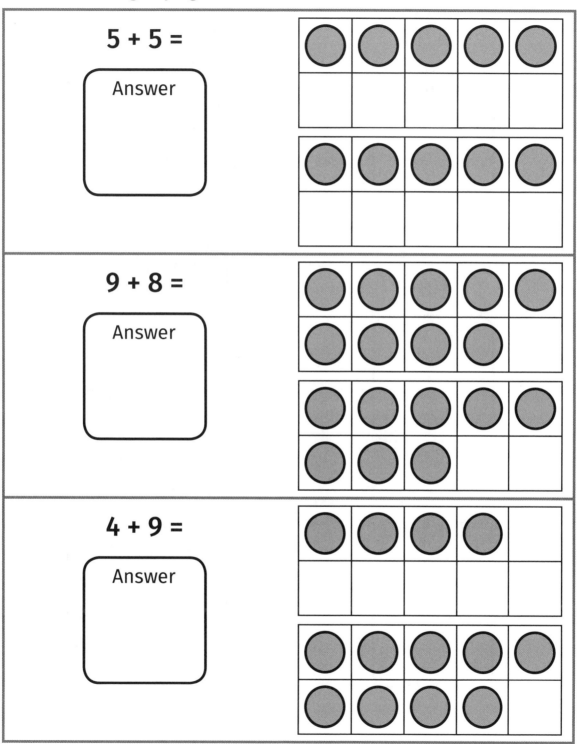

5 + 5 =

Answer

9 + 8 =

Answer

4 + 9 =

Answer

Addition with Regrouping on a Ten-Frame: Number Talks

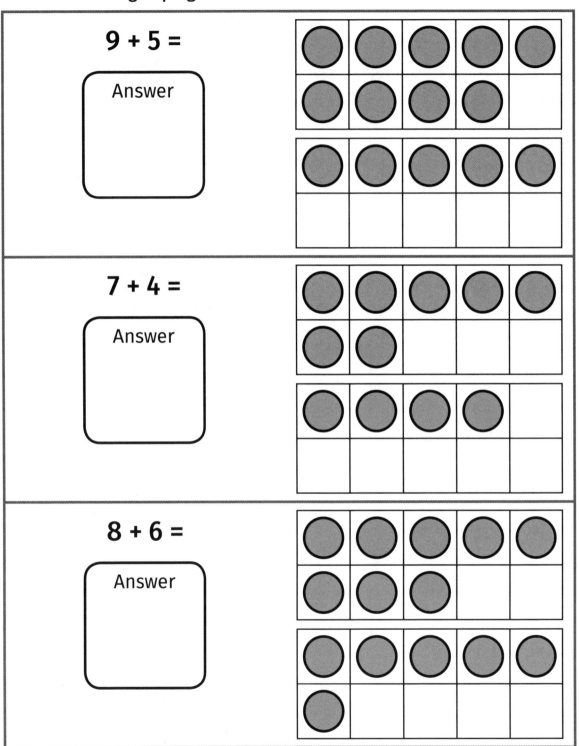

9 + 5 =

Answer

7 + 4 =

Answer

8 + 6 =

Answer

Addition with Regrouping on a Ten-Frame: Number Talks

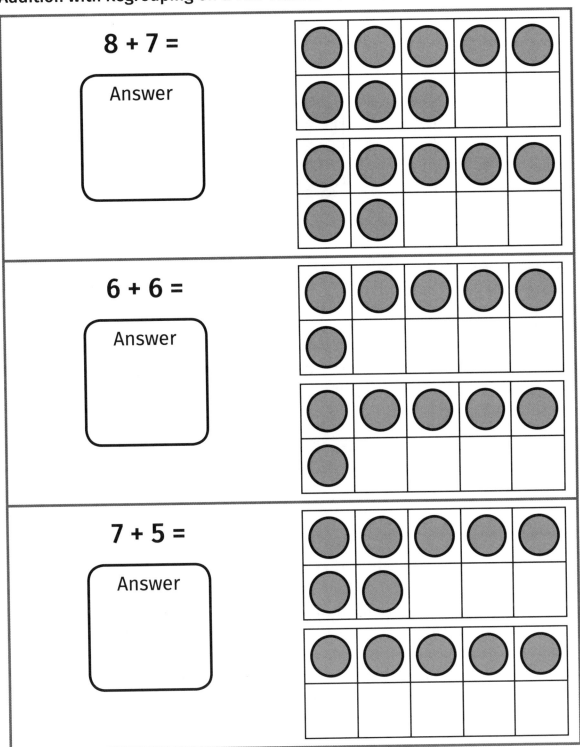

8 + 7 =

Answer

6 + 6 =

Answer

7 + 5 =

Answer

Subtraction on a Ten-Frame

What is 9 – 6?

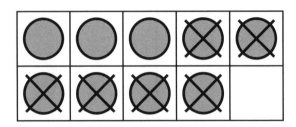

I see 1 ten-frame with 9 counters. I remove 6 by putting an X through them. Now I have 3 counters. 9 – 6 = 3.

TIPS

- Demonstrate this problem using a ten-frame and color counters.
- Give struggling students the color counters and a ten-frame to mirror the problem.

QUESTIONS

- What is 9 – 6? Use a thumbs-up when you have a solution.

- How many color counters did we start with? How many counters did we remove to find the answer? How many are left?

- What number is the minuend? Subtrahend? Difference?

- Can you explain the strategy you used to find the difference?

- Is there another strategy that works as well? Explain.

Subtraction on a Ten-Frame: Number Talks

3 − 2 =

Answer

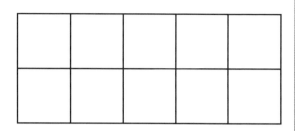

9 − 5 =

Answer

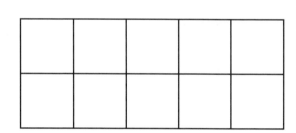

9 − 7 =

Answer

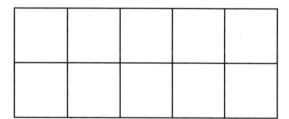

Subtraction on a Ten-Frame: Number Talks

8 – 6 =

Answer

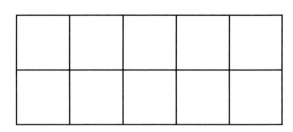

9 – 2 =

Answer

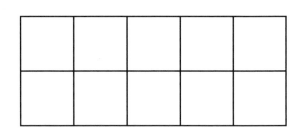

7 – 6 =

Answer

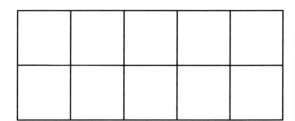

Subtraction on a Ten-Frame: Number Talks

8 – 2 =

Answer

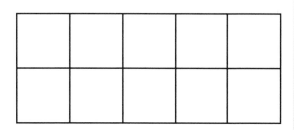

7 – 4 =

Answer

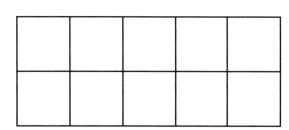

9 – 3 =

Answer

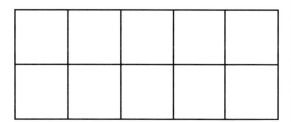

Addition: Looking for Doubles Using Connecting Cubes

What is 5 + 3?

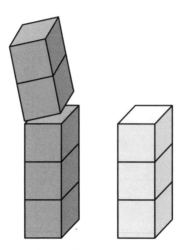

I can visualize doubles using connecting cubes. If I compare the 5 connecting cubes with the 3 connecting cubes, I see that they are both the same height at 3 cubes. So, I know that 3 and 3 are doubles. 3 and 3 is 6. I have 2 more cubes left over. 6 plus the 2 left over make 8 cubes. 5 + 3 = 8.

TIPS

• Using connecting cubes to show doubles and addition is great for beginning learners or students that need a visual.

• For struggling students, begin with small numbers or give them connecting cubes so they can mirror the problem.

QUESTIONS

• What is 5 + 3? Record student responses.

• What are doubles?

• How do you know these are doubles?

• How many extra cubes are there after you add these doubles?

• Does this help you understand addition? Explain.

• Can you add these using a different strategy?

Addition: Looking for Doubles Using Connecting Cubes: Number Talks

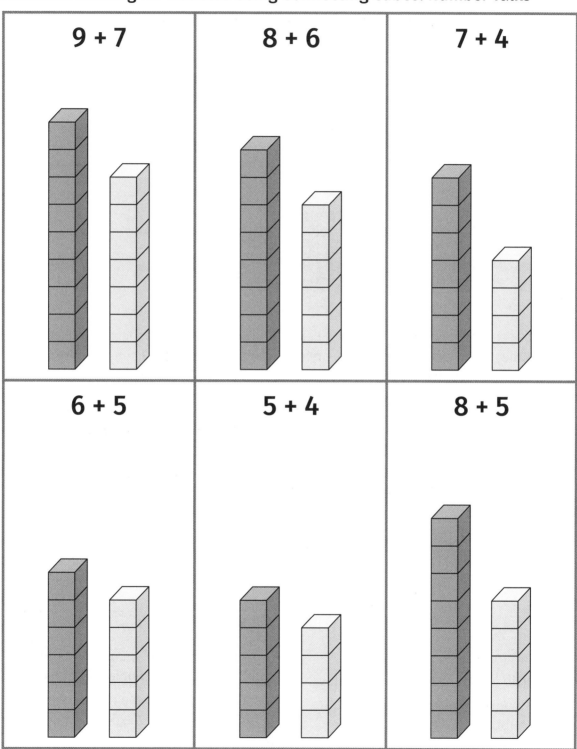

| 9 + 7 | 8 + 6 | 7 + 4 |
| 6 + 5 | 5 + 4 | 8 + 5 |

Subtraction: Looking for Doubles Using Connecting Cubes

EXAMPLE

What is 5 – 3?

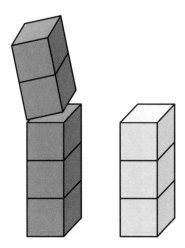

I can visualize doubles using connecting cubes. If I compare the 5 connecting cubes with the 3 connecting cubes, I see that they are both the same height at 3 cubes. So, I know that 3 and 3 are doubles. 3 minus 3 is 0. I still have 2 cubes left over. So, 5 – 3 = 2.

TIPS

- Using connecting cubes to show doubles and subtraction is great for beginning learners or students that need a visual.

- For struggling students, begin with small numbers or give them connecting cubes so they can mirror the problem.

QUESTIONS

- What are doubles?

- How do you know these are doubles?

- How many extra cubes are there after you subtract these doubles?

- How does this help you understand subtraction using doubles? Explain.

- Can you subtract these numbers using a different strategy? Explain.

Subtraction: Looking for Doubles Using Connecting Cubes: Number Talks

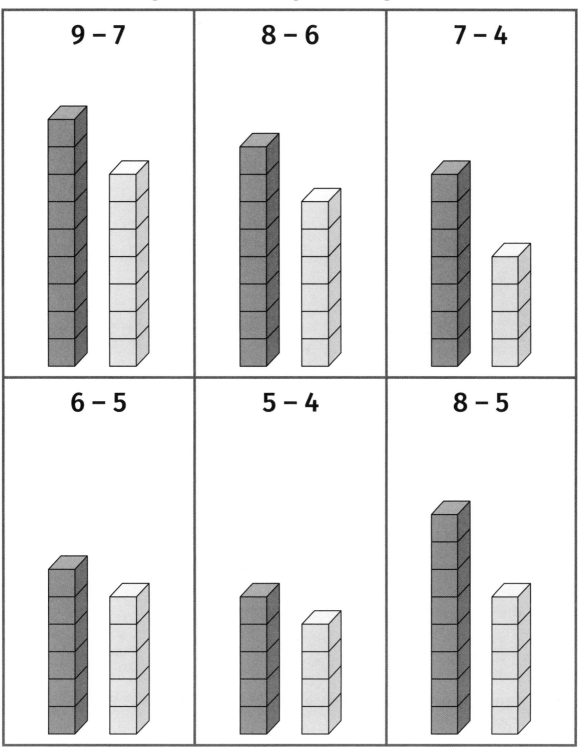

9 – 7	8 – 6	7 – 4
6 – 5	5 – 4	8 – 5

What Do You See?

I see 7 turtles. 4 are on the hill and 3 are waiting to climb the hill. I know that 4 and 3 more is 7.

TIPS

- Number talks help students verbalize their reasoning and explain their solutions.
- A number talk should be short and done daily. It should not take the place of core instruction.
- Have students tell you a counting story based on the picture.
- Welcome all responses from students.

QUESTIONS

- How many turtles can you count?
- Can you use a number line to show the total count?
- How many more turtles are needed to make 10?
- Are there more turtles on the hill or in the grass?

- What are the parts and what is the whole?
- If 3 turtles turned around and left the picture, how many would remain?
- What number sentence would match this story?

Mountain Climbing

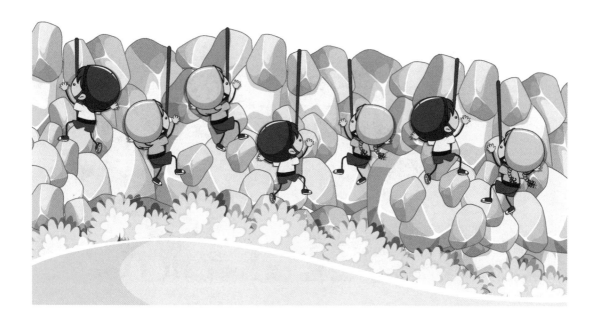

QUESTIONS

- How many climbers can you count?
- Can you use a number line to show the total count?
- How many climbers have dark gray hats?
- How many more light gray helmets are there than dark gray helmets?
- Can you show the total number of climbers on a ten-frame? What about with connecting cubes?

- How many more climbers are needed to make 10?
- Can you write a number sentence to show the parts and total?
- What numbers show parts of 7?
- Can you share a number story with the numbers 3, 4, and 7?

On the Farm

QUESTIONS

- How many children can you count?
- How many boys do you see?
- How many girls do you see?
- How many animals do you see?
- Are there more children than animals?
- Can you tell me a story about this picture?
- Can you write a number sentence to match your story?
- What are the parts in your number sentence? What is the whole?
- Can you show this using a number line or ten-frame?

Looking at Nine

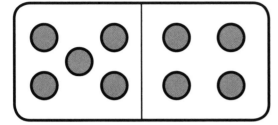

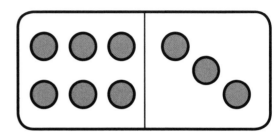

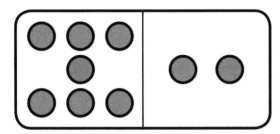

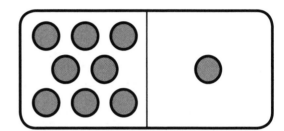

QUESTIONS

- How are these dominoes alike? How are they different?

- What is the whole in each of these dominoes?

- What are the parts in each of these dominoes?

- Can you use a number line to show the total count on each domino?

- How many more dots would it take to make a 10 for each of the dominoes?

- Can you write a number sentence for each domino?

- Can you tell a story about this picture?

Bus Stop

4 friends are on the bus.

2 are waiting to join them.

QUESTIONS

- What are the parts?
- What is the whole?
- Can you show this on a ten-frame or using connecting cubes?
- How many more friends would it take to make 10?
- How many fewer friends are waiting to get on the bus than are already on the bus?

- How many more friends are on the bus than waiting to board?
- Can you write a number sentence using the numbers 4, 2, and 6?
- If 3 friends got off the bus, how many would be left on the bus?

Seeing Double

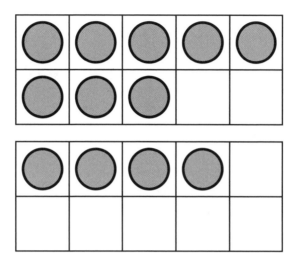

QUESTIONS

- What do you see?
- How many more counters are there than 10?
- How many groups of 10 are there?
- How many total counters do you see?
- What strategy did you use to find the sum of 8 and 4? Did you make a 10?
- How does making a 10 help you add?

- How can you show that 8 + 4 is the same as 10 + 2?
- Can you write a number sentence using the ten-frames?
- Can you model this with counters and ten-frames?

Part-Part-Whole

What is the missing part?

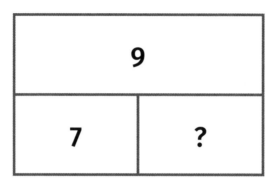

TIPS

- Have students find the missing part or whole.
- Ask students for a number sentence along with their thinking and strategy they used to find the missing numbers.
- Keep the mathematical practices in mind during a number talk.
- Number talks should be done separately from core instruction.

QUESTIONS

- What are the parts?
- What is the whole?
- How many more do you need to make a 9? Write a number sentence to describe this picture.
- What strategy can you use to find the missing part?
- What is the missing part?
- Can you tell me an addition story using the numbers 9, 7, and 2?
- Can you tell me a subtraction story using the numbers 9, 7, and 2?

Part-Part-Whole: Number Talks

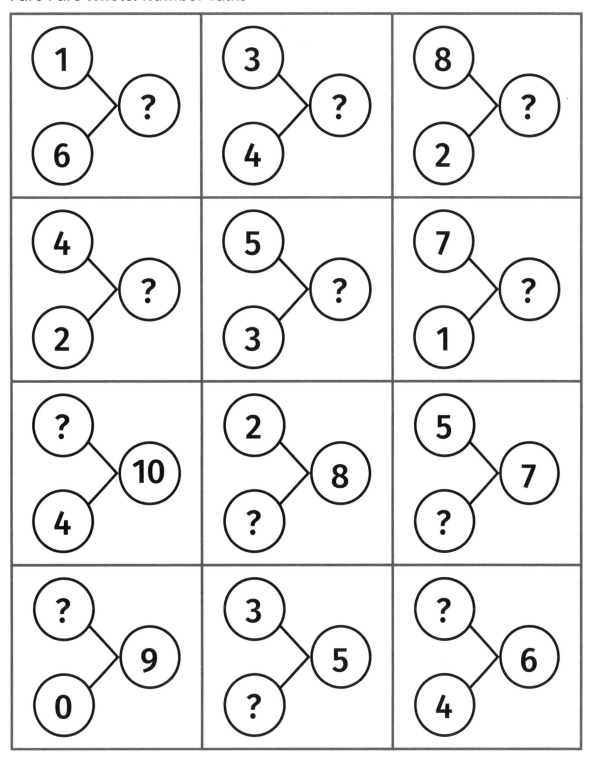

Adding on a Number Line: "Counting On" Strategy

What is 7 + 5?

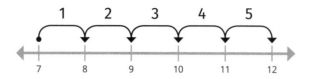

I begin at 7 and count up 5 more (or, I make 5 jumps) to reach 12. 7 + 5 = 12.

TIPS

- Using a number line will help students conceptually understand the relationship between numbers and strengthen their procedural fluency.
- For struggling students, begin with small numbers. If a student is still struggling, use concrete examples with color counters or connecting cubes.
- Always record student responses, including wrong answers, to showcase student thinking.

QUESTIONS

- What is 7 + 5? How can we show this using a number line?
- Does it matter which addend we start with on the number line?
- Why do we start with 7 and not 0? How does counting on work?
- Will you get the same answer if you add 7 + 5 or 5 + 7?
- How is this different or the same when using color counters or connecting cubes?
- Which strategy is more efficient?
- Can you explain this strategy in your own words? Can you explain it to a friend?

Adding on a Number Line: "Counting On" Strategy: Number Talks

2 + 9

5 + 6

10 + 3

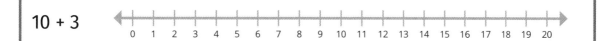

9 + 1

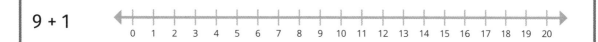

8 + 2

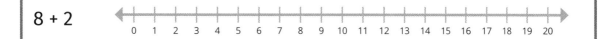

7 + 2

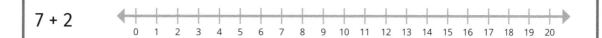

9 + 7

8 + 6

9 + 9

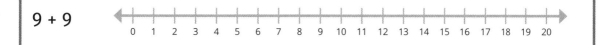

Subtracting on a Number Line: "Counting Back" Strategy

What is 9 – 5?

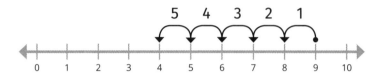

I start with the larger number, 9 (the minuend) on the number line, and I count back 5 jumps until I reach 4 (the subtrahend). The distance (or difference) between 9 and 5 is 4 units. 9 – 5 = 4.

TIPS

• It is important for students to visualize subtraction as the distance between two numbers. The difference between two numbers is their distance apart. In this problem, the distance or space between 9 and 5 is 4 units.

• Number talks should help students verbalize their reasoning and explain their solutions.

• Use errors to find additional strategies.

QUESTIONS

• What is 9 – 5? Record student responses.

• How can we show this using a number line?

• What is the minuend? What is the subtrahend? What is the difference?

• Does it matter which number we start with on the number line?

• Will you get the same answer if you subtract 9 – 5 or 5 – 9?

• What does the 4 represent?

• How is this different or the same when using color counters or connecting cubes?

• Which strategy is more efficient?

Subtracting on a Number Line: "Counting Back" Strategy: Number Talks

5 – 4

6 – 3

7 – 2

6 – 4

9 – 7

5 – 5

7 – 3

8 – 6

10 – 7

Subtracting on a Number Line: "Counting Up" Strategy

What is 8 – 3?

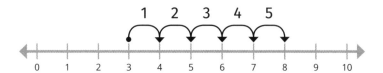

Start with the smaller number, 3 (the subtrahend) and count up until you reach the first number, 8 (the minuend). Notice it is 5 jumps, which is the distance (or difference) between 8 and 3.

TIPS

• It is important for students to visualize subtraction as the distance between two numbers. The difference between two numbers is their distance apart. In this problem, the distance or space between 8 and 3 is 5 units.

• Remember to welcome all responses from students.

• Celebrate thinking and understanding rather than answer-getting.

QUESTIONS

• What is 8 – 3? Record student responses.

• How can we show this using a number line?

• What is the minuend? What is the subtrahend? What is the difference?

• How is this different from counting back? Will you get the same answer?

• Is the difference and the distance between the two numbers the same?

• Can you explain your strategy in your own words?

• Can you think of another way to solve this problem?

Subtracting on a Number Line: "Counting Up" Strategy: Number Talks

9 – 1

5 – 5

7 – 1

6 – 2

10 – 3

9 – 2

6 – 4

7 – 6

8 – 6

Adding Groups of 10 on an Open Number Line

What is 50 + 30?

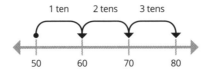

I start at 50 on an open number line. Since I am adding 30, which is the same as 3 groups of 10, I will jump on the number line by 3 groups of 10. 50 plus 10 is 60, 60 plus 10 more is 70, and 70 plus 10 more is 80. Therefore, 50 + 30 = 80.

TIPS

- Encourage conceptual explanations instead of procedural discussion.
- Teach students to respect each other's discussion points during a number talk.
- Record all student responses, even those that are incorrect.

QUESTIONS

- How can we show this using an open number line?

- Why use an open number line instead of a number line with all numbers between 0 and 80?

- How is this different from counting up? Will you get the same answer?

- Is the sum the same as the distance between the two numbers?

- Does everyone agree with this strategy?

- Can you explain the strategy in your own words?

Adding Groups of 10 on an Open Number Line: Number Talks

30 + 20	23 + 20
53 + 20	48 + 30
61 + 10	72 + 20
44 + 10	58 + 20
12 + 40	25 + 30
80 + 20	33 + 20

Subtracting Groups of 10 on an Open Number Line

What is 35 – 20?

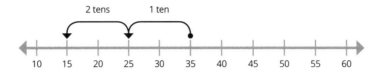

I start at 35. Since I am subtracting 20, which is 2 groups of 10, I will jump back on the number line by 2 groups of 10. 35 minus 10 is 25, and 25 minus 10 is 15. Therefore, 35 – 20 = 15.

TIPS

• It is important for students to visualize subtraction as the distance between two numbers. The difference between two numbers is their distance apart. In this problem, the distance or space between 35 and 20 is 15 units.

• Number talks offer a few minutes each day for students to build fluent retrieval of basic arithmetic skills.

• Record all student responses, even those that are incorrect.

QUESTIONS

• How can we show this using an open number line?

• Why use an open number line instead of a number line with all numbers between 0 and 35?

• How is this different from counting back? Will you get the same answer?

• Is the difference the same as the distance between the two numbers?

• Can you explain your strategy in your own words?

• Does everyone agree with this strategy?

Subtracting Groups of 10 on an Open Number Line: Number Talks

40 − 20	36 − 10
58 − 30	47 − 30
62 − 40	79 − 20
42 − 10	53 − 20
17 − 10	26 − 10
83 − 50	94 − 40

Ten More Using Base Ten Blocks

32 + 10 = ?

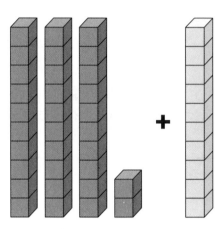

I see 3 groups of 10 with 2 ones next to it. I see another group of 10. If I put everything together, I have 4 tens and 2 ones. 32 + 10 = 42.

TIPS

- Kept in mind that we are building fluent retrieval of basic arithmetic facts.
- Number talks build on number sense and mathematical communication.
- Give struggling students base ten blocks and have them find the sum.

QUESTIONS

- What number is shown using base ten blocks?
- How many ones are shown?
- How many groups of 10 will be added?
- What is my total?
- Did the ones change at all?

- Is this strategy similar to another strategy?
- Do we all agree that the correct number of base ten blocks is…?

Ten More Using Base Ten Blocks: Number Talks

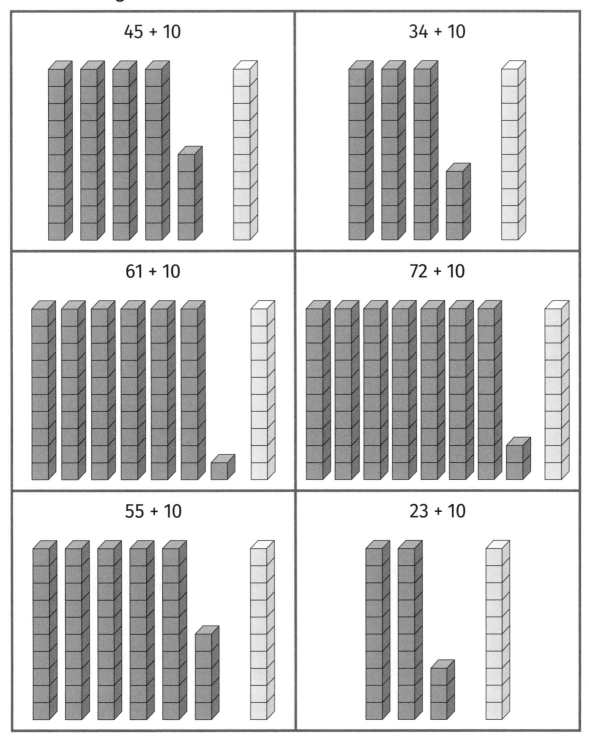

45 + 10

34 + 10

61 + 10

72 + 10

55 + 10

23 + 10

Ten Less Using
Base Ten Blocks

55 – 10 = ?

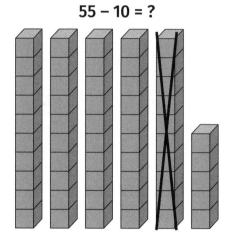

I see 5 groups of 10 and 5 ones. If I remove one group of 10, I am left with 4 groups of 10 and 5 ones. 55 – 10 = 45.

TIPS

• Ask students to explain their thought process.

• It takes time for students to become proficient with number talks. Don't give up!

• Students can more easily grasp a number talk when they repeat the strategy in their own words.

QUESTIONS

• What number is shown using base ten blocks?

• How many ones are shown? Did the ones change at all?

• How many groups of 10 will be removed?

• What is my total number?

• Is this strategy similar to another strategy?

• Can you explain your thinking?

• How does using base ten blocks help visualize subtraction?

• Can you prove your answer? How do you know you are right?

Ten Less Using Base Ten Blocks: Number Talks

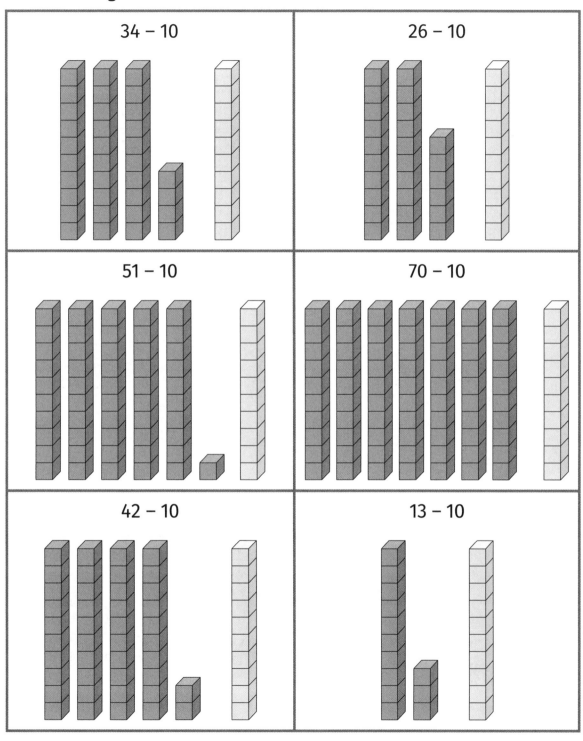

34 − 10

26 − 10

51 − 10

70 − 10

42 − 10

13 − 10

Addition: Jumps of 10 Using a Hundreds Chart

What is 32 + 22?

21	22	23	24	25	26	27	28	29	30
31	32	33	35	35	36	37	38	39	40
41	42	43	44	45	46	47	48	49	50
51	52	53	54	55	56	57	58	59	60

First, I can decompose one of the addends into groups of 10. 22 decomposes to 10 + 10 + 2. If I start at 32 on the hundreds chart, I can jump down by tens to find my answer. I jump by ten to 42, then another ten to 52. I have 2 ones left over, so I move to the right 2 places to my answer, 54.

TIPS

- Give struggling students a hundreds chart and have them use color counters to jump to the answer.

QUESTIONS

- Why decompose the 22 to 2 groups of 10 and 2 ones?

- Does it help to see this on a hundreds chart?

- What is the sum of 32 and 22?

- How can jumps of 10 help you add quickly?

- Could we decompose the first addend to groups of 10? Would that change our sum?

- Where would we start on the hundreds chart if we decomposed 32 instead of 22? How many jumps of 10 would you make? What about the 1s?

- Would a number line show this same sum?

Addition: Jumps of 10 Using a Hundreds Chart: Number Talks

1	2	3	4	5	6	7	8	9	10
11	12	13	14	15	16	17	18	19	20
21	22	23	24	25	26	27	28	29	30
31	32	33	35	35	36	37	38	39	40
41	42	43	44	45	46	47	48	49	50
51	52	53	54	55	56	57	58	59	60
61	62	63	64	65	66	67	68	69	70
71	72	73	74	75	76	77	78	79	80
81	82	83	84	85	86	87	88	89	90
91	92	93	94	95	96	97	98	99	100

23 + 35	41 + 53	14 + 36
36 + 42	13 + 43	22 + 45
26 + 12	33 + 16	35 + 21
48 + 30	53 + 24	56 + 14
64 + 24	74 + 13	82 + 15

Subtraction: Jumps of 10 Using a Hundreds Chart

What is 56 – 31?

21	22	23	24	25	26	27	28	29	30
31	32	33	35	35	36	37	38	39	40
41	42	43	44	45	46	47	48	49	50
51	52	53	54	55	56	57	58	59	60

I can decompose the subtrahend, 31, into 3 groups of 10 and 1 one: 10 + 10 + 10 + 1. Starting at 56 on the hundreds chart, I jump up 3 rows of 10 to get 26. I have 1 remaining, so I move to the left 1 place to get the answer: 25.

TIPS

- Give struggling students the hundreds chart and have them use color counters to jump to the answer.
- Make sure to help students understand that with subtraction, the jumps are back or up on the hundreds chart while addition is adding to or jumps forward and down on the hundreds chart.
- For struggling learners, step back to a number line or a manipulative such as snap cubes/color counters to show the operation.

QUESTIONS

- What do you see?
- Why decompose the 31 into 3 groups of 10 and a 1?
- Does it help to see this on a hundreds chart?
- What is the difference between 56 and 31?
- How do jumps of 10 help you subtract quickly?
- Could we decompose the first number into groups of 10 and ones and find the right answer? Explain.

Subtraction: Jumps of 10 Using a Hundreds Chart: Number Talks

1	2	3	4	5	6	7	8	9	10
11	12	13	14	15	16	17	18	19	20
21	22	23	24	25	26	27	28	29	30
31	32	33	35	35	36	37	38	39	40
41	42	43	44	45	46	47	48	49	50
51	52	53	54	55	56	57	58	59	60
61	62	63	64	65	66	67	68	69	70
71	72	73	74	75	76	77	78	79	80
81	82	83	84	85	86	87	88	89	90
91	92	93	94	95	96	97	98	99	100

18 − 14	25 − 22	27 − 15
34 − 12	39 − 25	44 − 21
46 − 32	53 − 20	58 − 34
64 − 32	66 − 43	76 − 33
87 − 25	95 − 41	92 − 25

Working with Fives

What is 9 + 8?

(4 + 5) + (5 + 3)

4 + 5 + 5 + 3

(4 + 3) + 10 = 17

I can decompose the numbers to make addition easier. Decompose by looking for 5s. The 9 decomposes to 5 + 4 and the 8 decomposes to 5 + 3. Now, I can add the 5s to make 10, and the 4 and 3 to make 7. Addition by 10 is now easy. I can add 10 to 7 to find my answer of 17.

TIPS

- Through a number talk, students are taught the relationship between numbers, which makes computational fluency easy.
- If students struggle to decompose numbers and make 10s, step back to a more concrete strategy.
- Help struggling students by using manipulatives such as color counters, base ten blocks, and connecting cubes.

QUESTIONS

- What do you see?
- Why can we decompose both numbers using 5 as one of the numbers?
- How does this make addition easier?
- What numbers would you group together to add more quickly?
- What is the answer to 9 + 8?
- Can you show this using a ten-frame? Is the answer still the same?

Working with Fives: Number Talks

7 + 6	10 + 6	11 + 9
7 + 8	6 + 6	12 + 7
6 + 8	8 + 8	11 + 6
9 + 7	8 + 7	11 + 8
7 + 9	8 + 9	6 + 7
6 + 12	9 + 6	6 + 9
7 + 7	7 + 9	9 + 8
9 + 9	9 + 11	9 + 12

Adding Using Known Facts

What is 40 + 30?

I know that 4 + 3 is 7. I also know that 4 tens and 3 tens is the same as 7 tens. Therefore, 40 + 30 = 70.

TIPS

- Using known facts helps when adding groups of 10s.
- All students must agree on the correct answer.
- Do a number talk every day. The more you do number talks, the better students become at conceptually understanding mathematics.

QUESTIONS

- What is your estimate for adding 40 + 30?
- How can adding the 10s help you find an answer quickly?
- Is there another strategy that will help you prove your answer?

- Can you share your strategy with a friend? Explain your thinking.
- How does this work?
- Can you prove your answer another way? Explain.

Adding Using Known Facts: Number Talks

30 + 20	40 + 10	10 + 40
10 + 30	60 + 10	20 + 10
50 + 30	80 + 20	10 + 50
30 + 30	40 + 20	30 + 10
10 + 80	10 + 70	20 + 20
20 + 50	60 + 20	70 + 20
30 + 40	30 + 50	60 + 30
40 + 60	50 + 50	50 + 40

Subtracting
Using Known Facts

What is 50 – 20?

I know that 5 – 2 is 3. I also know that 5 tens – 2 tens is the same as 3 tens. Therefore, 50 – 20 is 30.

TIPS

- Using known facts helps when subtracting groups of 10s.
- Ask a few students to share their thinking and strategies.
- Record all responses, even incorrect answers. Come to a consensus once all strategies have been shared.

QUESTIONS

- What is your estimate when subtracting 20 from 50?
- How can subtracting the 10s help you find an answer quickly?
- Is there another strategy that will help you prove your answer?

- Can you share your strategy with a friend? Explain your thinking.
- How does this work?
- Can you prove your answer another way? Explain.

Subtracting Using Known Facts: Number Talks

30 − 20	40 − 10	70 − 40
50 − 30	20 − 10	80 − 10
40 − 30	60 − 10	90 − 50
30 − 30	40 − 20	70 − 30
90 − 30	80 − 50	80 − 40
70 − 50	60 − 40	60 − 30
50 − 10	40 − 30	30 − 10
90 − 40	80 − 60	70 − 20

Adding by Making 10

What is 8 + 9?

(7 + 1)

7 + 1 + 9

7 + 10 = 17

I can decompose the numbers to make addition easy. I will look to make a 10. 8 decomposes to 7 and 1. I can group the 1 with the 9 to make a 10. Now I have 10 and 7. 10 + 7 is 17.

TIPS

- You can also decompose the 9 to 7 + 2 so you can make a 10 with 8 + 2.
- Making a 10 is an important strategy that will help students with future math. It is a building block for computational fluency with all operations.
- If students are not successful with decomposing numbers and making 10s, step back to a more concrete strategy.
- Help struggling students by using manipulatives such as color counters, base ten blocks, and connecting cubes.

QUESTIONS

- What is 8 + 9? Record student responses.
- If you decompose the 9 instead of the 8, how would that look? What numbers will help you make a 10?
- What strategy did you use? Explain.
- Does this strategy make sense? Can you explain this strategy to a friend?
- What is the correct answer to this problem?
- Can you share a number story using 8 + 9?

Adding by Making 10: Number Talks

7 + 4 =

↓ decompose

_____

↓

_____ = _____

8 + 6 =

↓ decompose

_____

↓

_____ = _____

9 + 9 =

↓ decompose

_____

↓

_____ = _____

6 + 9 =

↓ decompose

_____

↓

_____ = _____

9 + 7	5 + 9	8 + 9
7 + 8	9 + 3	8 + 5
5 + 8	8 + 4	7 + 5
6 + 7	6 + 6	6 + 5

Add by Using Doubles

What is 8 + 9?

(8 + 1)

8 + 8 + 1

16 + 1 = 17

Doubles are easy to remember. I can decompose 9 into 8 and 1, so now I have double of 8. Now I can add the doubles, 8 and 8, to get 16, and add the 1 to get 17.

TIPS

• Using facts students already know, such as doubles, makes addition easy.

• If this strategy is difficult, use color counters or connecting cubes to show doubles.

• Accept any strategy as long as it is correct.

• Record student responses.

QUESTIONS

• What is 8 + 9?

• What are doubles?

• How can I make doubles with 8 and 9? Which number will decompose to help you?

• How can you prove your answer is correct?

• How can you explain your thinking?

• Can addends be grouped in any order to get the same sum?

• Why do you have to double the smaller addend instead of the larger addend?

Add by Using Doubles: Number Talks

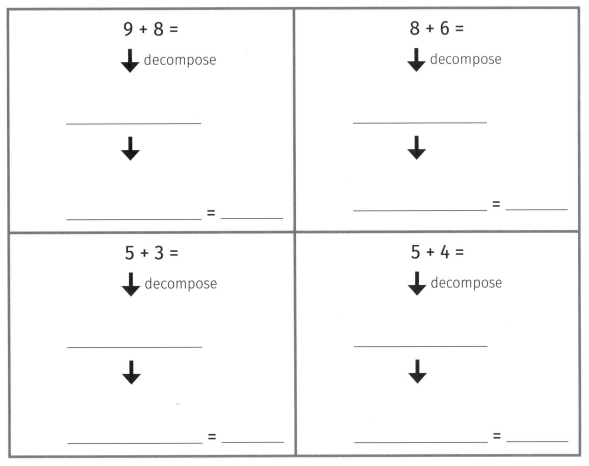

9 + 8 =

↓ decompose

_____

↓

_____ = _____

8 + 6 =

↓ decompose

_____

↓

_____ = _____

5 + 3 =

↓ decompose

_____

↓

_____ = _____

5 + 4 =

↓ decompose

_____

↓

_____ = _____

10 + 9	5 + 6	6 + 4
5 + 8	6 + 8	7 + 8
9 + 5	7 + 5	5 + 11
9 + 6	6 + 7	8 + 9

Subtract by Using Doubles

What is 7 – 6?

(6 + 1)

1 + (6 – 6)

1 + 0 = 1

Doubles are easy to remember. I can decompose 7 to 6 and 1. Now I have a double of 6. 6 minus 6 is 0, and 0 plus 1 is 1.

TIPS

- Using facts students already know, such as doubles, makes subtraction easy.
- If this strategy is difficult, use color counters or connecting cubes to show doubles.
- Accept any strategy as long as it is correct.
- Record student responses.

QUESTIONS

- What is 7 – 6?
- What do you see?
- Does looking for a double make subtraction easier?
- After subtracting the doubles, what was remaining?

- Why does changing the numbers to doubles help you quickly subtract?
- Can you show this on a number line? What about a ten-frame?

Subtract by Using Doubles: Number Talks

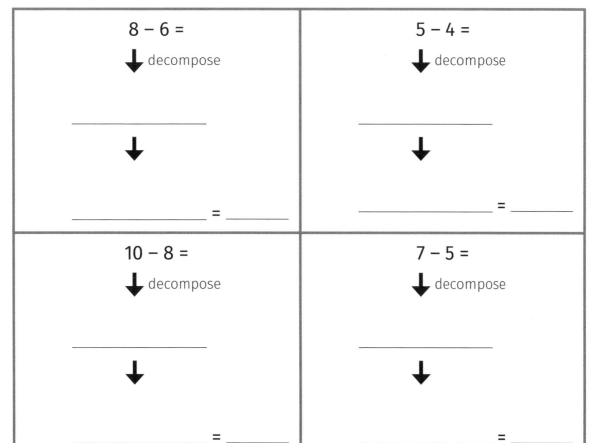

8 − 6 =

↓ decompose

_____

↓

_____ = _____

5 − 4 =

↓ decompose

_____

↓

_____ = _____

10 − 8 =

↓ decompose

_____

↓

_____ = _____

7 − 5 =

↓ decompose

_____

↓

_____ = _____

10 − 9	10 − 7	8 − 5
5 − 3	9 − 6	9 − 7
8 − 7	7 − 4	5 − 3
9 − 8	6 − 5	10 − 6

Related Addition Facts

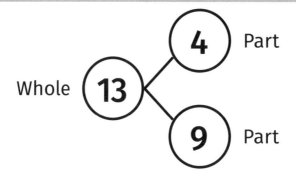

Whole **13** — **4** Part

9 Part

I can use number bonds to see the relationship between addition and subtraction. Using my understanding of part-part-whole, I can write related number sentences.

Related facts
4 + 9 = 13
9 + 4 = 13
13 − 9 = 4
13 − 4 = 9

TIPS

- This exercise is about looking for the relationship between addition and subtraction.
- For struggling learners, use manipulatives such as color counters or connecting cubes to show the related facts.

QUESTIONS

- How are these numbers related?
- How do you know…?
- Can you explain this?
- How can you show this using manipulatives?

- How are addition and subtraction related?
- What is the whole and what are the parts?

Related Addition Facts: Number Talks

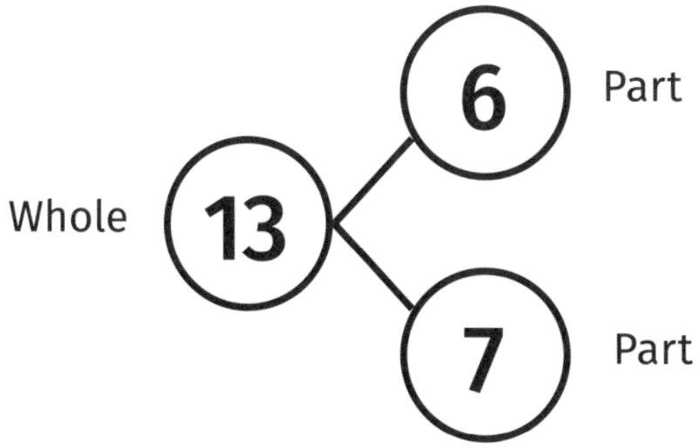

Related Facts

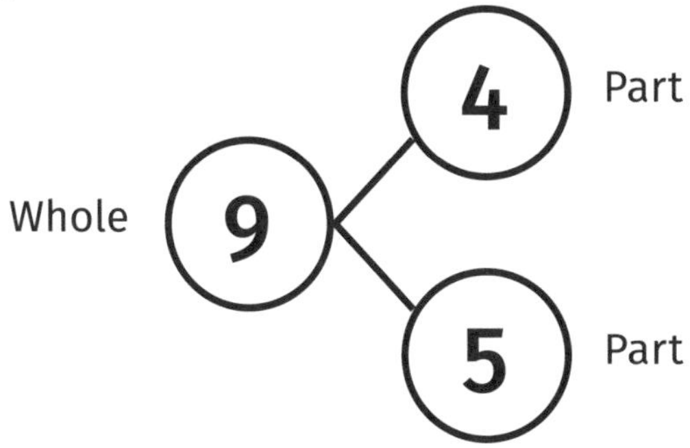

Whole **13** Part **6** Part **7**

_____

_____

_____

_____

Related Facts

Whole **9** Part **4** Part **5**

_____

_____

_____

_____

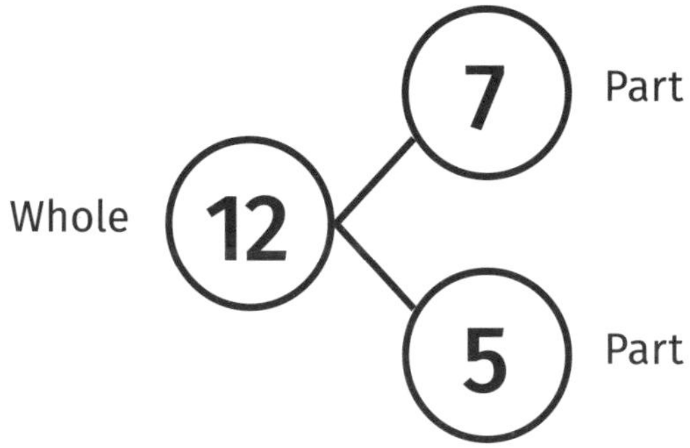

Related Facts

Whole **12** Part **7** Part **5**

_____

_____

_____

_____

Related Addition Facts: Number Talks

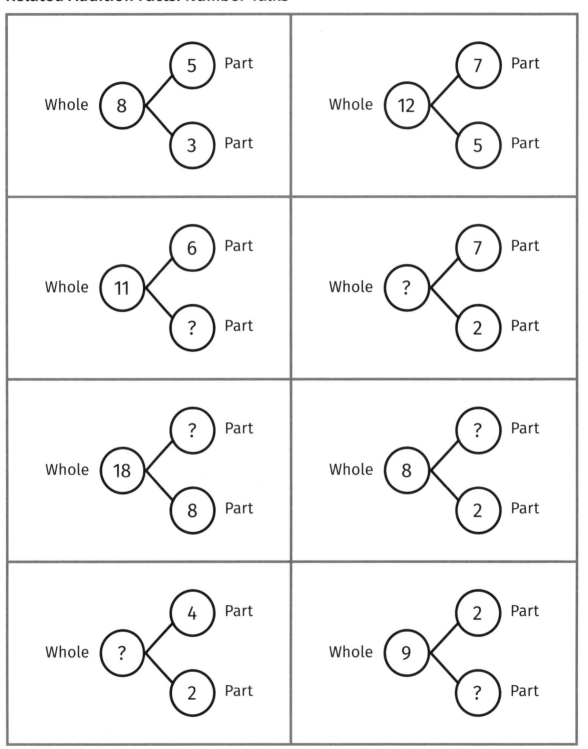

Whole 8 — 5 Part, 3 Part

Whole 12 — 7 Part, 5 Part

Whole 11 — 6 Part, ? Part

Whole ? — 7 Part, 2 Part

Whole 18 — ? Part, 8 Part

Whole 8 — ? Part, 2 Part

Whole ? — 4 Part, 2 Part

Whole 9 — 2 Part, ? Part

Adding Tens and Ones

What is 28 + 6?

(2 + 4)

(28 + 2) + 4

30 + 4

I look for numbers that can make groups of 10s. First, I decompose the 6 to 2 + 4. Then, I add the 2 to 28 to get 30. Now I have 3 groups of 10. I have 4 more 1s remaining. 30 + 4 = 34.

TIPS

- Keep mathematical practices in mind during a number talk.
- If the strategy is difficult, step back to smaller numbers or use base ten blocks to show the addition.
- If a student's answer contains a mistake, allow the student to revise their initial answer.

QUESTIONS

- What is the solution to this addition problem?
- Which addend is easier to decompose to find a group of 10?
- What numbers work best when decomposing the addend?
- Why use 2 and 4 when decomposing 6 instead of 3 and 3?
- Is this strategy similar to another strategy you know?
- Can you describe your strategy?
- What would be a good estimate of the answer?

Adding Tens and Ones: Number Talks

33 + 9	46 + 8	18 + 4
17 + 6	29 + 5	26 + 6
57 + 4	68 + 3	19 + 3
37 + 5	48 + 7	38 + 7
19 + 8	25 + 7	34 + 8
46 + 9	57 + 7	66 + 9
72 + 8	87 + 6	16 + 7
28 + 9	39 + 6	47 + 5

Grade 2

The purpose of a number talk is to promote computational fluency. These number talks will focus on key standards that require fluency, as outlined on page 6. In second grade, the proficiency standards are 2.OA.B.2 and 2.NBT.B.5. Standards that support fluency with addition and subtraction within 20 using mental math strategies and within 100 based on place value, properties of operations and relationships between addition and subtraction are all included in these number talks.

The following strategies align to second grade standards and are essential for conceptual understanding leading to procedural fluency.

2.OA.A.1 Use addition and subtraction within 100 to solve one- and two-step word problems involving situations of adding to, taking from, putting together, taking apart, and comparing, with unknowns in all positions, e.g., by using drawings and equations with a symbol for the unknown number to represent the problem.

2.OA.B.2 Fluently add and subtract within 20 using mental strategies. By end of Grade 2, know from memory all sums of two one-digit numbers.

2.OA.C.3 Determine whether a group of objects (up to 20) has an odd or even number of members, e.g., by pairing objects or counting them by twos; write an equation to express an even number as a sum of two equal addends.

2.OA.C.4 Use addition to find the total number of objects arranged in rectangular arrays with up to five rows and up to five columns; write an equation to express the total as a sum of equal addends.

2.NBT.B.5 Fluently add and subtract within 100 using strategies based on place value, properties of operations, and/or the relationship between addition and subtraction.

2.NBT.B.6 Add up to four two-digit numbers using strategies based on place value and properties of operations.

2.NBT.B.7 Add and subtract within 1000, using concrete models or drawings and strategies based on place value, properties of operations, and/or the relationship between addition and subtraction; relate the strategy to a written method. Understand that in adding or subtracting three-digit numbers, one adds or subtracts hundreds and hundreds, tens and tens, ones and ones; and sometimes it is necessary to compose or decompose tens or hundreds.

2.NBT.B.8 Mentally add 10 or 100 to a given number 100–900, and mentally subtract 10 or 100 from a given number 100–900.

2.NBT.B.9 Explain why addition and subtraction strategies work, using place value and the properties of operations. (Explanations may be supported by drawings or objects.)

In this section are the following addition strategy examples with suggested number talks:

Addition Using Base Ten Blocks

What is 36 + 22?

	Tens	Ones	Solve
36	(3 tens rods)	(6 ones cubes)	I have a total of 5 tens (30 + 20), and 8 ones (6 + 2). **36 + 22 = 58**
22	(2 tens rods)	(2 ones cubes)	

I see that my first addend has 3 groups of 10 and my second addend has 2 more groups of ten, for a total of 5 groups of ten, or 50. I see that my first addend has 6 ones and my second addend has 2 ones, for a total of 8 ones. I add my 5 tens and my 8 ones. 50 + 8 = 58.

TIPS

• Number talks should be a daily routine.

• If the student is struggling, give the student base ten blocks to mirror the problem.

• If a student is struggling, use easier numbers.

QUESTIONS

• What addition problem is shown?

• How many different strategies can you think of to find the sum?

• Share your strategy with your neighbor. Was their thinking different from yours?

• How do base ten blocks help you visualize and understand addition of two-digit numbers?

• How do you know your solution is correct?

Addition Using Base Ten Blocks: Number Talks

45 + 34
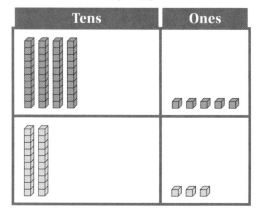

62 + 22
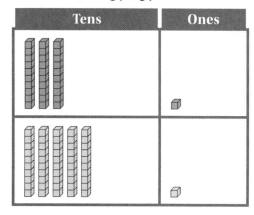

45 + 23

<table>
<tr><th>Tens</th><th>Ones</th></tr>
</table>

31 + 51

52 + 36

37 + 42
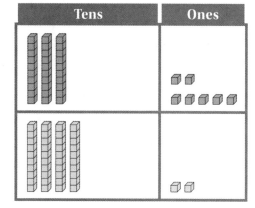

Addition with Regrouping Using Base Ten Blocks

What is 53 + 38?

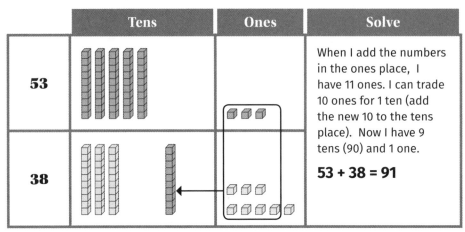

	Tens	Ones	Solve
53			When I add the numbers in the ones place, I have 11 ones. I can trade 10 ones for 1 ten (add the new 10 to the tens place). Now I have 9 tens (90) and 1 one.
38			**53 + 38 = 91**

I see that the first addend has 5 groups of ten (50) and the second addend has 3 more groups of ten (30), for a total of 8 groups of ten. I have 3 ones in the first addend and 8 ones in the second addend, for a total of 11 ones. I can trade 10 of the ones for a ten. Now I have 9 tens (90) and 1 one for a sum of 91. 53 + 38 = 91.

TIPS

- A number talk will help students move from memorizing a standard algorithm to making sense of mathematics.
- Mistakes are all part of the learning process. Use them as a teaching tool.
- A number talk should help students recall prior mathematical knowledge.
- Multiple strategies and representations are discovered through a number talk.

QUESTIONS

- What do you see?
- How can you use base ten blocks to show regrouping?
- Can you explain this strategy in your own words?
- How would you explain regrouping?
- When do you know you need to regroup?
- What would happen if you didn't regroup?

Addition with Regrouping Using Base Ten Blocks

55 + 38

Tens	Ones

66 + 27

Tens	Ones

46 + 28

Tens	Ones

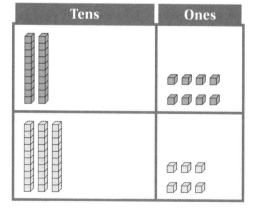

39 + 54

Tens	Ones

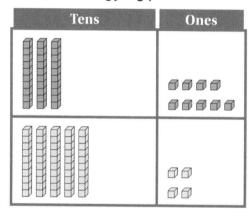

28 + 36

Tens	Ones

47 + 35

Tens	Ones

Subtraction Using
Base Ten Blocks

What is 55 – 34?

	Tens	Ones	Solve
55	(base ten blocks)	(base ten blocks)	I know I need to subtract 3 tens (30) from the tens column and 4 ones from the ones column. 5 tens (50) minus 3 tens (30) leaves me with 2 tens (20). When I subtract 4 ones from 5 ones, I am left with 1 one. When I do this, I am left with 21.
34	(base ten blocks)	(base ten blocks)	**55 – 34 = 21**

I see that my minuend has 5 tens (50) and 5 ones (5) and my subtrahend has 3 tens (30) and 4 ones (4). I subtract the 3 tens from the tens column and 4 ones from the ones column. When I do this, I am left with 2 tens and 1 one. This means that the difference between 55 and 34 is 21.

TIPS

• Base ten blocks are a first step in helping students understand addition and subtraction. Notice in this problem, we are not regrouping.

• Keep number talks short. They should be 5 to 10 minutes in duration. Be careful if your number talks continue longer than they should.

• A number talk should not replace core instruction.

QUESTIONS

• What subtraction problem is shown? What do you see?

• Do you have a strategy to solve this problem?

• Do you need to regroup in this problem?

• How do you know...? What happens if...?

• How do you show this on a number line?

• Is this strategy efficient?

Subtraction Using Base Ten Blocks: Number Talks

65 − 33

Tens	Ones

74 − 42

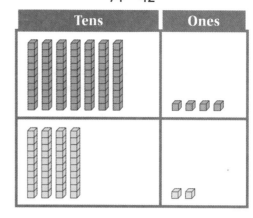

49 − 16

Tens	Ones

86 − 43

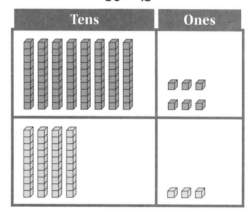

57 − 22

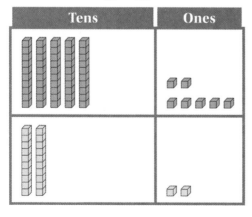

38 − 21

Tens	Ones

Subtraction with Regrouping Using Base Ten Blocks

What is 63 – 48?

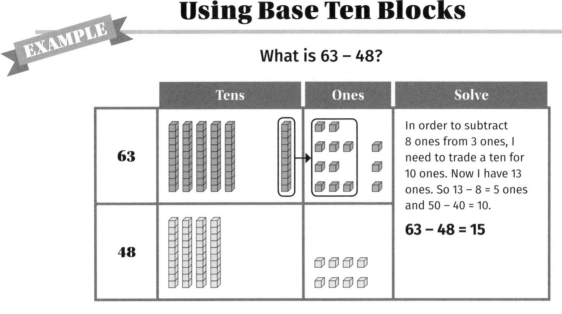

	Tens	Ones	Solve
63			In order to subtract 8 ones from 3 ones, I need to trade a ten for 10 ones. Now I have 13 ones. So 13 – 8 = 5 ones and 50 – 40 = 10. **63 – 48 = 15**
48			

I see that the minuend has 6 tens (60) and 3 ones and the subtrahend has 4 tens (40) and 8 ones. In order to subtract 8 ones from 3 ones, I need to trade a ten for 10 ones. Ten ones and 3 more ones makes 13 ones, which gives me enough to subtract 8 ones. 13 – 8 = 5. Then, I subtract the tens: 5 tens (50) – 4 tens (40) leaves me with 1 ten (10). I add the differences together: 5 + 10 = 15. So, 63 – 48 = 15.

TIPS

- When designing a number talk, think about basic skills your students need.
- When doing number talks, use problems that a student will not only be successful with but also have multiple pathways to solve.
- Make sure to write down student thinking so students can see the structure of their mathematical thinking.

QUESTIONS

- What subtraction problem is shown? What do you see?
- Do you have a strategy to solve this problem?
- Explain how regrouping with base ten blocks works.
- How would you describe your strategy?
- How many strategies can you think of to solve this problem? Explain.
- How could you show this on a number line?

Subtraction with Regrouping Using Base Ten Blocks: Number Talks

54 – 36

Tens	Ones

73 – 46

Tens	Ones

34 – 16

Tens	Ones

62 – 27

Tens	Ones

46 – 28

Tens	Ones

83 – 56

Tens	Ones

Addition on Ten-Frames

What is 17 + 12?

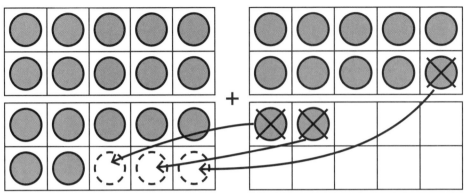

First, I filled in the ten-frames on the left with 17 counters. Then, I filled in the ten-frames on the right with 12 counters. I can add efficiently by making groups of 10. To do this, I move 3 counters from the right frame over to the ten-frames on the left to make a group of 10. Now, I have 2 tens on the left and 9 ones on the right. It is easy to add 20 and 9. 20 + 9 = 29.

TIPS

- Give struggling students color counters and ten-frames to mirror the problem.
- Make sure to have students explain why the strategy they selected works and makes sense.
- Remind students that they should not be using paper or pencils; number talks should be mental math.
- Have students share while you record student responses.

QUESTIONS

- Which strategy did you use to find your sum? Share your thinking.
- If I switched the addends, would the sum still be the same?
- Does anyone have a different strategy?
- How many counters are used to make a group of ten with the first addend?
- How can you prove your sum using a number line? Explain.

Addition on Ten-Frames: Number Talks

11 + 14	13 + 16	14 + 15
12 + 15	13 + 17	12 + 13
12 + 17	11 + 17	14 + 16
13 + 15	12 + 11	11 + 16
11 + 15	18 + 11	12 + 14
17 + 18	15 + 17	16 + 16
18 + 16	19 + 14	17 + 14
15 + 16	18 + 13	19 + 13

Subtraction on Ten-Frames

What is 23 – 15?

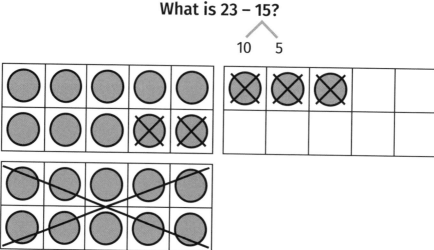

I have 23 counters in my ten-frame. I want to subtract 15 counters. I know that 15 is the same as 1 group of 10 and 5 ones. I remove 1 group of 10, and I know that 5 can be decomposed to 3 and 2. I remove 3 counters to get to 10, then I remove 2 more. There are 8 counters remaining; this is the difference. 23 – 15 = 8.

TIPS

• Give struggling students color counters and ten-frames to mirror the problem.

• If the problem is too difficult, step back to smaller numbers.

• Record student strategies for all students to see.

• If need be, help clarify student's strategy.

QUESTIONS

• Why is it important to decompose the subtrahend?

• What strategy did you use to find your difference? Share your thinking. Record student responses.

• If I switched the minuend and subtrahend, would the difference still be the same? Explain.

• Does anyone have a different strategy they want to share?

• How can you explain this strategy in your own words? Share with your neighbor.

• Can you prove your answer using a number line? Explain.

Subtraction on Ten-Frames: Number Talks

25 – 17	33 – 21	45 – 36
19 – 14	29 – 18	37 – 22
46 – 28	17 – 12	27 – 16
36 – 28	26 – 13	32 – 14
28 – 19	42 – 19	24 – 15
35 – 21	48 – 14	22 – 12
39 – 24	43 – 18	42 – 27
29 – 14	44 – 23	38 – 16

Addition Using Place Value Strips

What is 54 + 23?

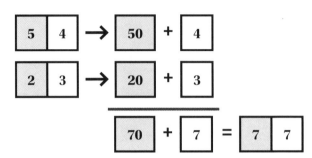

I can show addition using place value strips. I start by constructing 54 and 23 using place value strips. Then, I expand the numbers to show the tens and ones. Now I can add the tens (50 + 20) and the ones (4 + 3). My sum is 77.

TIPS

- Using place value strips is a wonderful way to represent numbers that can be easily added or subtracted using expanded form.
- If a student struggles with place value strips, step back to base ten blocks or color counters.
- A number talk will reinforce and strengthen mathematical practice.
- Number talks can help students find a strategy or pathway to a solution that makes sense to them.
- Discussing, analyzing, conjecturing, and discovering helps students make sense of math.

QUESTIONS

- What strips do you use to make your numbers?
- What are the numbers in expanded form?
- Which numbers are the tens and which are the ones?
- How do you add these numbers?
- What strategy did you use?
- What is the solution to this problem?
- How is this similar to using base ten blocks?
- How can you explain this strategy in your own words?

Addition Using Place Value Strips: Number Talks

16 + 13	38 + 11	25 + 24
29 + 40	44 + 23	32 + 42
37 + 42	13 + 26	45 + 34
55 + 23	27 + 32	48 + 31
52 + 16	65 + 13	62 + 11
24 + 24	31 + 54	44 + 35
63 + 13	54 + 32	51 + 26
23 +25	34 + 25	61 + 37

Addition with Regrouping Using Place Value Strips

EXAMPLE

What is 52 + 29?

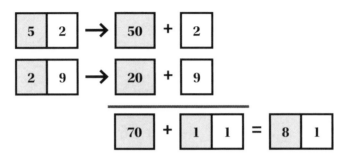

I can show addition with regrouping using place value strips. I start by constructing 52 and 29 using place value strips. I can expand the numbers to show the tens and ones. Now I can add the tens (50 + 20) and the ones (9 + 2). When I add the ones, I make 11, which is a ten and a one. When I add my tens (50 + 20 + 10) and my ones (1), I get 81.

TIPS

- A number talk will help students become more precise with numbers.
- By using a number talk, students communicate and use the words and symbols of math to explain their mathematical strategies.
- Students use their own words to calculate a correct answer and explain how they did the math.
- Number talks are mental math; they should not be done with pencil and paper.

QUESTIONS

- What is your estimated answer?
- How do place value strips show regrouping?
- How can you explain regrouping using place value strips to a friend? Explain.
- What numbers did you need to regroup?
- How do you know you need to regroup?
- What is the answer to this problem?
- How do place value strips help you visualize addition?

Addition with Regrouping Using Place Value Strips: Number Talks

12 + 19	23 + 28	35 + 38
44 + 48	52 + 29	26 + 49
24 + 57	15 + 28	38 + 43
58 + 19	34 + 47	43 + 29
16 + 37	47 + 28	68 + 15
57 + 16	37 + 25	48 + 17
28 + 19	65 + 27	39 + 39
45 + 27	66 + 28	59 +26

Subtraction Using Place Value Strips

What is 58 – 14?

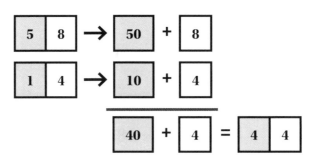

I can show subtraction using place value strips. I start by constructing 58 and 14 using place value strips. I can expand the numbers to show the tens and ones. Now I can subtract the tens (50 – 10) and the ones (8 – 4). The difference is 44.

TIPS

• Using place value strips, students can easily see how to subtract two or more digit numbers. By pulling apart the place value strips, students can see the place value of each number, which will aid in conceptual understanding.

• Place value strips will help students identify the position of the numerical digit.

• Encourage students to support their understanding using mathematical vocabulary.

QUESTIONS

• How can you describe the problem and your strategy in your own words? Explain.

• What do you notice?

• Are there other problems like this that you have tried? Explain.

• What do these numbers represent?

• How would you demonstrate an example of this problem?

• How would you explain your strategy to a friend?

• Can you describe a number story based on these numbers?

Subtraction Using Place Value Strips: Number Talks

25 – 12	49 – 34	28 – 17
46 – 23	36 – 25	55 – 32
37 – 15	57 – 43	27 – 13
66 – 41	76 – 52	39 – 22
85 – 52	69 – 47	98 – 74
78 – 36	65 – 32	58 – 35
35 – 23	48 – 27	28 – 16
77 – 43	47 – 15	59 – 46

Subtraction with Regrouping Using Place Value Strips

What is 51 – 26?

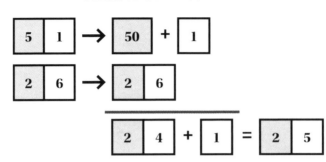

Using place value strips, I can show subtraction with regrouping. I begin by constructing both the minuend and subtrahend using place value strips. Expanding the strips, I see that 50 becomes 50 + 1 and 26 becomes 20 + 6. Since I do not have enough ones to subtract 6, I will not expand the 26 to tens and ones but leave it as 26. I subtract 50 – 26 to 24 and add on the remaining 1.

TIPS

• I can use place value strips to subtract when I have to regroup. Place value strips help students understand the need to regroup when you do not have enough ones to subtract.

• Require precise vocabulary when discussing and sharing strategies.

• If necessary, help students find patterns to solve a mathematical problem.

QUESTIONS

• How do you know that your answer is reasonable?

• Is there another strategy that works better to solve this problem?

• How can you prove your answer?

• Will this strategy always work? Explain.

• Is there a better strategy to solve this problem?

Subtraction with Regrouping Using Place Value Strips: Number Talks

43 – 18	25 – 16	36 – 28
42 – 25	55 – 37	64 – 46
78 – 59	88 – 59	93 – 75
34 – 28	46 – 19	53 – 27
66 – 48	74 – 56	84 – 66
41 – 28	23 – 19	33 – 19
60 – 35	72 – 46	35 – 27
51 – 48	22 – 14	53 – 17

Adding by Tens
on a Hundreds Chart

What is 29 + 20?

10 10

21	22	23	24	25	26	27	28	29	30
31	32	33	35	35	36	37	38	39	40
41	42	43	44	45	46	47	48	49	50
51	52	53	54	55	56	57	58	59	60

I can visualize addition quickly using a hundreds chart. There are 2 tens in 20. I start at 29 and jump by 1 group of 10 to get to 39, then by another group of 10 to get to 49. 29 + 20 = 49.

TIPS

- Remind students that a jump down on a hundred chart is adding by a group of ten just as a jump up would be subtracting a group of 10.

- If a student needs clarification, count by ones until you get to ten more or ten less.

- Through a number talk, students understand that numbers can be composed and decomposed to make new numbers.

- Focus on the mathematical practices during number talks.

- During number talks, students should construct viable arguments and critique the reasoning of others.

QUESTIONS

- What is your estimated answer to the problem?

- Why decompose the second addend to two groups of ten?

- Does it help to see this on a hundreds chart?

- How do jumps of 10 help you add quickly?

- Could you decompose the first number to groups of 10? Would that change your sum?

- Would a number line show this same sum? Explain.

Adding by Tens on a Hundreds Chart: Number Talks

16 + 30	22 + 30	44 + 20
41 + 40	58 + 30	35 + 40
28 + 20	15 + 40	53 + 20
34 + 30	47 + 30	12 + 20
67 + 20	24 + 60	39 + 20
17 + 20	25 + 30	38 + 30
36 + 40	42 + 30	62 + 20
55 + 20	57 + 20	27 + 40

Subtracting by Tens on a Hundreds Chart

What is 84 – 40?

10 10 10 10

31	32	33	35	35	36	37	38	39	40
41	42	43	44	45	46	47	48	49	50
51	52	53	54	55	56	57	58	59	60
61	62	63	64	65	66	67	68	69	70
71	72	73	74	75	76	77	78	79	80
81	82	83	84	85	86	87	88	80	90

I can subtract quickly using a hundreds chart. First, I decompose 40 to 4 tens (10 + 10 + 10 + 10). Then, I find 84 on the hundreds chart. 84 minus 1 group of ten takes me to 74, another jump of 10 takes me to 64, another takes me to 54, and my last jump of 10 takes me to the difference, which is 44. 84 – 40 = 44.

TIPS

- The use of a hundreds chart is ideal for helping students understand subtraction by groups of 10.
- Use a number line to help struggling students.
- It is important for all students to come to an agreement on the correct solution to the problem.

QUESTIONS

- What is your estimated answer to the problem? Is it the same as the final answer?
- Do you agree or disagree with your classmate's answer? Why?
- Does it help to see this on a hundreds chart?
- How do jumps of 10 help you subtract quickly?
- How can you prove you are right?
- Explain this strategy in your own words.
- How do you show this on a number line?

Subtracting by Tens on a Hundreds Chart: Number Talks

98 − 30	78 − 40	88 − 30
66 − 30	55 − 20	92 − 50
73 − 50	51 − 40	83 − 20
86 − 60	95 − 40	64 − 20
69 − 40	58 − 30	75 − 30
48 − 20	77 − 20	89 − 50
85 − 40	62 − 50	63 − 30
94 − 20	39 − 10	57 − 30

Adding Tens and Ones

What is 53 + 24?

21	22	23	24	25	26	27	28	29	30
31	32	33	35	35	36	37	38	39	40
41	42	43	44	45	46	47	48	49	50
51	52	53	54	55	56	57	58	59	60
61	62	63	64	65	66	67	68	69	70
71	72	73	74	75	76	77	78	79	80

I can decompose 24 into 20 + 4, which is the same as 2 tens and 4 ones. I can find the sum by jumping down on the number line by 2 groups of 10 and then moving right by 4 ones. Starting at 53, I jump down 2 groups of 10 to 73 and move right by 4 ones to 77. 53 + 24 = 77.

TIPS

• Using a hundreds chart is a natural segue from adding with manipulatives. Students can visually see how easy it is to add by groups of tens and ones.

• Number talks help students explore their thinking and conjectures. They allow students to make their arguments based on drawings, diagrams, charts, strategies, or manipulatives.

• Number talks make math sing!

QUESTIONS

• What answer did you get?

• How can you prove your answer is correct?

• How can you show your answer using a different strategy?

• Is there a strategy you like better?

• What would this look like on a number line?

• What would happen if you added the ones first, then the tens? Would you get the same answer?

Adding Tens and Ones: Number Talks

18 + 26	23 + 25	35 + 35
44 + 24	32 + 21	46 + 31
28 + 24	15 + 32	48 + 19
51 + 31	34 + 52	22 + 62
17 + 44	57 + 36	51 + 22
53 + 23	25 + 18	18 + 21
36 + 36	48 + 25	61 + 14
37 + 29	74 + 24	67 + 22

Subtracting Tens and Ones

What is 67 – 44?

21	22	23	24	25	26	27	28	28	30
31	32	33	35	35	36	37	38	39	40
41	42	43	44	45	46	47	48	49	50
51	52	53	54	55	56	57	58	59	60
61	62	63	64	65	66	67	68	69	70
71	72	73	74	75	76	77	78	79	80

I begin subtracting at the minuend, 67. I jump down 4 rows or 4 groups of 10 to 27. Now, I need to subtract the 4 ones. I jump 4 spaces left to 23. So, my difference, or the distance between the two numbers, is, 23.

TIPS

- Discussion, sharing, and analysis empower students with mathematical knowledge.
- It is important that students find a strategy that makes sense to them.
- It is important for students to share their strategies, and hopefully, the students will find strategies they understand and that work well for them during the appropriate situation.

QUESTIONS

- What is your estimated answer for this problem?
- How do you find the difference between ____ and ____ on a hundreds chart?
- Why do you start with the smaller number?
- Why do you count by ones to match the ones in ____?
- How many spaces to the left is ____ from ____?

- Why do you count by tens to ____?
- How many rows down from ____ is ____? How many tens is that?
- How many tens and ones are between ____ and ____ ?
- What is the difference or distance between the two numbers?
- Why is the difference and distance the same number? Explain.

Subtracting by Tens and Ones on a Hundreds Chart: Number Talks

72 − 39	85 − 37	94 − 52
66 − 38	57 − 16	82 − 46
96 − 47	78 − 52	61 − 42
84 − 58	51 − 14	98 − 61
63 − 53	77 − 26	59 − 29
75 − 43	49 − 16	54 − 18
35 − 28	81 − 64	37 − 22
44 − 12	95 − 38	68 − 44

Addition: Jumps of Tens and Ones on a Number Line

EXAMPLE

What is 38 + 27?

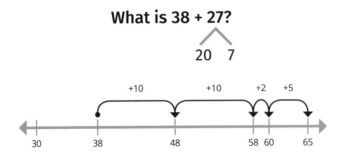

To solve this problem, I decomposed the addend 27 to 20 + 7, which is an equivalent expression. This means that 27 is equivalent to 20 + 7. On an open number line, I can add quickly by using jumps of 20 or 2 jumps of 10. Then, I jump by 7, or by 2 + 5, which are friendly numbers. 38 plus a jump of 10 takes me to 48 and another jump of 10 brings me to 58. Adding 2 will take me to 60 and then 5 more is 65, my sum.

TIPS

- If the problem is too difficult, step back to smaller numbers.
- Use manipulatives such as base ten blocks for students struggling with this pictorial representation.
- Help students share their answers and strategies in a productive, respectful manner. Record all answers, even if some are incorrect.
- Remind students that comprehending is more than following a procedure. Make sure all students can verbalize their reasoning strategies.

QUESTIONS

- Can you think of a different strategy for solving this problem?
- Which addend did you decompose? Where did you start on the number line?
- What jumps did you make on the number line to get your answer?
- If you decomposed the other addend, would you still get the same answer?

Addition: Jumps of Tens and Ones on a Number Line: Number Talks

54 + 21	18 + 28	39 + 42
24 + 29	43 + 41	64 + 35
71 + 26	16 + 47	21 + 15
37 + 37	51 + 34	88 + 12
49 + 18	67 + 25	71 + 29
62 + 32	17 + 32	35 + 35
26 + 18	73 + 42	81 + 41
19 + 45	59 + 27	42 + 28

Subtraction: Counting Down by Tens and Ones on a Number Line

What is 45 − 23?

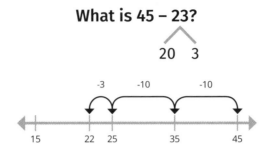

First, I decomposed the subtrahend 23 to 20 + 3, which is an equivalent expression. Starting at the minuend, 45, I can subtract quickly on an open number line by jumping back 2 groups of 10 to get 25, and then jumping back the remaining 3 ones. If I jump back 1 group of 10 from 45, I get 35, and another jump of 10 takes me to 25. My final jump of 3 ones puts me at 22. 45 − 23 is 22.

TIPS

- Having students explain their thinking is more important than arriving at an answer.
- Value all student responses, even incorrect responses.
- Give students the opportunity to self-correct errors if needed.
- When you facilitate the number talk, model a strategy if needed.
- For struggling learners, step back to smaller numbers.

QUESTIONS

- Did you decompose the minuend or subtrahend? Explain.
- Does it matter which number you decompose?
- Will you get the same answer if you decompose the minuend instead of the subtrahend?

- Is there another strategy you can use?
- How does using an open number line help you subtract quickly and efficiently?

Subtraction: Counting Down by Tens and Ones on a Number Line: Number Talks

19 – 13	27 – 16	59 – 41
15 – 9	39 – 26	29 – 16
48 – 25	26 – 14	67 – 48
53 – 28	34 – 17	88 – 72
75 – 24	46 – 23	62 – 46
28 – 14	37 – 23	45 – 38
59 – 41	64 – 31	77 – 46
82 – 54	73 – 36	84 – 63

Subtraction: Counting Up on a Number Line by Tens and Ones

What is 76 − 35?

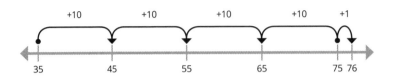

I can count up from the subtrahend to subtract. I start with my subtrahend, 35, and count the number of jumps it will take to reach the minuend, 76. I jump by 4 tens to 75, then I need to jump an additional 1 unit to get to 76. Now, I add my jumps, or the distance between 35 and 76, to find the difference. 10 + 10 + 10 + 10 + 1 = 41. The distance between 35 and 76 is 41.

TIPS

- Use student errors to explore other strategies that will work.
- Keep in mind that mistakes are all part of the learning process.
- All students should have a voice during a number talk.
- Repeat student strategies out loud to make sure everyone understands the method that was used to solve the problem.
- For struggling learners, step back to smaller numbers.

QUESTIONS

- How is this similar or different from counting back on a number line?
- Which strategy is easier to understand—counting up or counting back?
- What strategy did you use? How can you describe your strategy to your neighbor? Explain.
- Does everyone agree on the correct answer?
- How do you know your answer is correct? Explain.

Subtraction: Counting Up on a Number Line by Tens and Ones: Number Talks

17 – 13	38 – 25	26 – 15
54 – 37	42 – 38	61 – 46
28 – 17	39 – 16	75 – 26
48 – 33	85 – 38	57 – 33
74 – 43	66 – 35	84 – 55
19 – 8	27 – 14	36 – 19
45 – 34	56 – 38	68 – 47
72 – 24	88 – 57	59 – 36

Subtraction Using Friendly Numbers on a Number Line

What is 56 – 39?

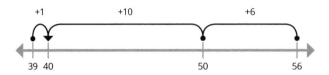

To solve this problem mentally, I look for friendly numbers that will give me the difference between 56 and 39. On an open number line, I start with the subtrahend, 39, and jump 1 unit to 40, a nice friendly number. I can jump another 10 units to get to 50, another friendly number. All I need is 6 more jumps to get to the minuend, 56. Now I know that the difference between 39 and 56 is 1 + 10 + 6, or 17.

TIPS

• Use student errors to explore other strategies that will work.

• Before a number talk begins, ask for possible solutions.

• Remind students to estimate the solution before sharing strategies.

• For struggling learners, step back to smaller numbers.

QUESTIONS

• What strategy did you use to solve this problem?

• How does using friendly numbers help you subtract quickly?

• How can you restate this strategy in your own words? Share with your neighbor.

• Is this strategy similar to another strategy you have used?

• Is this an efficient strategy? How does it work?

Subtraction Using Friendly Numbers on a Number Line: Number Talks

38 – 29	47 – 35	25 – 47
28 – 19	58 – 36	66 – 45
75 – 48	34 – 28	87 – 53
48 – 27	62 – 46	56 – 38
89 – 68	96 – 65	73 – 24
26 – 15	37 – 23	45 – 28
59 – 42	64 – 38	77 – 52
83 – 29	92 – 26	97 – 58

Subtraction Using Equivalent Expressions

EXAMPLE

What is 48 – 36?

What is 50 – 38?

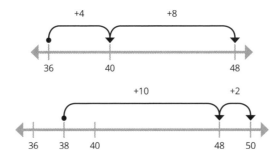

If I add or subtract the same number from both the minuend or the subtrahend, the difference, or distance between the two numbers, will not change. For example, I know that 48 – 36 equals 12. If I add 2 to both the minuend and the subtrahend, to get 50 – 38, the distance between both numbers will still be 12. Therefore, 48 – 36 and 50 – 38 are equivalent expressions. They are the same even though they look different because they will give you the same value.

TIPS

- A number talk helps students initiate a strategy to solve mathematics. Help students find a correct strategy by using good question prompts.

- Require students to give feedback and provide evidence to support their pathway to a solution.

- Ask students to find a pattern that might be in the problem that will help them discover a pathway to a solution.

QUESTIONS

- Does this strategy make sense?
- How can you explain these 2 problems in your own words?
- How are the expressions alike and how are they different?

- What do you notice about both expressions?
- How does the number line help you explain the solution?
- Will it still work if you subtracted 2 from the minuend and subtrahend?

Subtraction Using Equivalent Expressions: Number Talks

56 − 34 53 − 31	19 − 12 20 − 13	68 − 42 70 − 44
33 − 21 32 − 20	58 − 29 60 − 31	40 − 18 39 − 17
43 − 28 38 − 23	28 − 13 26 − 11	15 − 8 19 − 12
45 − 17 40 − 12	50 − 19 49 − 18	67 − 18 70 − 21
88 − 59 89 − 60	72 − 46 70 − 44	26 − 17 29 − 20

Adding to Subtract

What is 78 – 39?

Add 1 to the minuend: 78 + 1 = 79

Add 1 to the subtrahend: 39 + 1 = 40

79 – 40 = 39, so 78 – 39 = 39

I can quickly solve a subtraction problem by adding the same number to both the minuend and subtrahend. I add 1 to both numbers to make a new problem, 79 – 40. It is easy to subtract 40 from 79. Visualizing this problem on a number line, I have only changed the position on the number line, not the distance between the numbers subtracted. My answer is 79 – 40 = 39. This means 78 – 39 = 39.

TIPS

- Number talks build conceptual understanding so that a student uses an algorithm; it makes mathematical sense.
- Focus on conceptual understanding so procedures become quick, efficient, and understandable.
- We add to subtract to make computation efficient and easy.

QUESTIONS

- How do you describe your strategy?
- How else could you solve this problem?
- What evidence do you have to support your solution?
- How can you test your solution to see if you are right?
- How would you explain your strategy to a friend?

Adding to Subtract: Number Talks

67 – 23	90 – 69	51 – 28
48 – 18	77 – 46	82 – 65
36 – 28	29 – 16	18 – 13
23 – 14	39 – 23	41 – 32
59 – 25	62 – 26	79 – 51
19 – 12	27 – 18	98 – 59
83 – 49	73 – 39	68 – 47
55 – 38	46 – 28	33 – 27

Adding by Decomposing
to Tens and Ones

What is 68 + 27?

60 8 20 7

Add the tens: 60 + 20 = 80

Add the ones: 8 + 7 = 15

80 + 15 = 95

I can mentally solve an addition problem by decomposing the addends into tens and ones. For this problem, I decompose the first addend to 6 tens and 8 ones, and the second addend to 2 tens and 7 ones. I add the tens (60 + 20 = 80) and add my ones (8 + 7 = 15). My answer will be the sum of 80 + 15, which is 95.

TIPS

• This is an abstract strategy. If students have difficulty with abstract reasoning, step back to a representational method such as a number line or a concrete method with manipulatives such as base ten blocks.

• Always start with smaller numbers if students are struggling.

• Have students investigate their strategy before sharing with the class.

• Number talks help make sense of mathematics.

• A number talk can help you discover student misconceptions.

QUESTIONS

• What strategy did you use?

• What information did you need to solve this problem?

• What do you estimate to be the solution?

• Would a manipulative help you solve this problem?

• Is there another strategy you could use to find an answer?

• What are the tens and the ones?

• How does adding by tens and ones help you mentally find your answer?

Adding by Decomposing to Tens and Ones: Number Talks

45 + 34	26 + 28	17 + 17
63 + 26	34 + 25	55 + 28
14 + 81	42 + 45	23 + 62
37 + 19	53 + 41	77 + 22
74 + 14	68 + 15	86 + 9
13 + 47	28 + 53	36 + 42
44 + 51	56 + 38	67 + 15
72 + 23	32 + 54	46 + 22

Subtracting by Decomposing to Tens and Ones

What is 46 − 14?

40 6 10 4

Subtract the tens: 40 − 10 = 30

Subtract the ones: 6 − 4 = 2

30 + 2 = 32

I can mentally solve a subtraction problem by decomposing both the minuend and subtrahend into tens and ones. For this problem, I decompose the minuend into 4 tens and 6 ones, and I decompose the subtrahend into 1 ten and 4 ones. Once I have my tens and ones, I subtract the tens (40 − 10 = 30) and subtract my ones (6 − 4 = 2). My answer will be the sum of 30 + 2, which is 32.

TIPS

- This is an abstract strategy. If students have difficulty with abstract reasoning, step back to a representational method such as a number line or a concrete method with manipulatives such as base ten blocks.
- A number talk is about productive struggle and being able to justify, clarify, and discuss mathematics.
- Students should be rephrasing, discussing, critiquing, analyzing, and reflecting during a number talk.
- Number talks are for all students. Even struggling students should find an entry point to solving mathematics.

QUESTIONS

- What strategy did you use?
- What are the tens and the ones?
- How does using tens and ones help you mentally find your answer?
- Would this strategy be efficient if the minuend had fewer ones than the subtrahend? Why?

Subtracting by Decomposing to Tens and Ones: Number Talks

38 − 24	18 − 12	47 − 31
17 − 14	55 − 32	26 − 14
29 − 15	37 − 16	64 − 31
46 − 23	57 − 42	78 − 62
66 − 45	85 − 62	96 − 64
16 − 13	27 − 15	38 − 23
49 − 34	58 − 26	65 − 51
77 − 53	89 − 45	93 − 41

Adding in Expanded Form

What is 63 + 28?

6 tens + 3 ones

+ 2 tens + 8 ones
_____

8 tens + 11 ones = 91

I can mentally solve this addition problem by writing both addends, 63 and 28, in expanded form. 63 is 60 + 3, and 28 is 20 + 8. Writing the expressions in vertical form, I add the tens and then the ones. 60 + 20 is 80 and 3 + 8 is 11. Now all I have to do is add 80 and 11 to give me the sum of 91.

TIPS

- This is an abstract strategy. If students have difficulty with abstract reasoning, step back to a representational method such as a number line or a concrete method with manipulatives such as base ten blocks.
- Have another student repeat the strategy used.
- Refer to the mathematical practices, listed on page 7, during a number talk.
- Avoid procedural responses. Number talks should encourage conceptual thinking.
- Students should clarify and express their thinking with mathematical language.

QUESTIONS

- What is your estimated answer to this problem?
- How does a place value strategy help you mentally add numbers?
- Is it easy to add in expanded form?

- Do you need to regroup when adding in expanded form?
- Is there another adding strategy that is just as easy? Do both strategies give you the same answer?

Adding in Expanded Form: Number Talks

26 + 25	48 + 39	33 + 27
67 + 23	71 + 26	82 + 12
19 + 48	29 + 18	45 + 38
37 + 31	15 + 18	64 + 37
24 + 35	78 + 19	28 + 28
34 + 46	37 + 28	46 + 25
58 + 25	52 + 37	62 + 14
76 + 21	72 + 17	33 + 26

Subtracting in Expanded Form

What is 47 − 25?

4 tens + 7 ones

− 2 tens + 5 ones

2 tens + 2 ones = 22

I can mentally solve this subtraction problem by writing both minuend and subtrahend, 47 and 25, in expanded form. 47 in expanded form is 40 + 7, and 25 in expanded form is 20 + 5. Writing the expressions in vertical form, I subtract the tens and then the ones. 40 − 20 is 20 and 7 − 5 is 2. Now I add 20 and 2 to give me the difference of 22.

TIPS

- Subtraction is easy to understand when using place value. If the student struggles with expanded form, move back to using a concrete method such as base ten blocks.

- Have students predict how subtraction would work in expanded form with regrouping. The discussion, conjectures, and predictions are a great way to get students thinking and talking about math.

- A number talk is a great instructional strategy where students can enjoy mathematics in a nonthreatening environment.

QUESTIONS

- What is your estimated answer to this problem?

- How does a place value strategy help to mentally subtract?

- Is it easy to subtract in expanded form?

- What do you predict we would need to do if we didn't have enough ones to subtract?

- Is there another strategy where it is just as easy to subtract these two numbers? Do both strategies give you the same answer?

Subtracting in Expanded Form: Number Talks

24 – 13	47 – 32	38 – 22
59 – 34	36 – 21	67 – 45
37 – 16	27 – 13	49 – 26
25 – 14	69 – 51	56 – 42
58 – 42	44 – 13	76 – 45
23 – 42	28 – 15	46 – 24
42 – 31	54 – 22	58 – 37
66 – 24	67 – 25	32 – 22

Subtracting in Expanded Form with Regrouping

What is 68 − 39?

$$\begin{array}{l} \overset{5}{\cancel{6}} \text{ tens} + \overset{18}{\cancel{8}} \text{ ones} \\ -\ 3 \text{ tens} + 9 \text{ ones} \\ \hline 2 \text{ tens} + 9 \text{ ones} = 29 \end{array}$$

In this problem, my minuend, 68, has more ones than my subtrahend, 39. I can regroup in expanded form to make subtracting easier. This requires that I trade in a group of ten for 10 ones so subtraction will work. I expand my minuend into 6 tens and 8 ones, then trade 1 ten for 10 ones. Now I have 5 tens and 18 ones. I can subtract in expanded form to find my answer.

TIPS

- Regrouping can be difficult for struggling learners. If a student is having difficulty, use base ten blocks and smaller numbers to show the operation.
- Number talks are essential for showing students that there are multiple ways to solve a problem. This is important for student understanding of mathematics.
- Number talks teach number sense, which helps students make sense of math.
- Sharing strategies helps students clarify their thinking.

QUESTIONS

- How is this like addition with regrouping? How is it different?
- What is your thinking?
- What is your estimated answer?
- What numbers need to be traded so you can regroup?
- What do you not understand about this strategy?
- Can you explain your strategy to your neighbor?

Subtracting in Expanded Form with Regrouping: Number Talks

35 − 18	42 − 26	53 − 27
65 − 38	51 − 42	72 − 54
43 − 18	34 − 27	67 − 49
75 − 47	54 − 38	41 − 15
31 − 28	66 − 38	84 − 66
23 − 15	24 − 18	32 − 16
44 − 29	52 − 36	63 − 47
61 − 35	60 − 28	73 − 36

Compensation to Add

What is 48 + 19?

48 + 19

-1   +1
‾‾‾‾‾‾‾
47 + 20 = 67

I can mentally solve this addition problem by using compensation. I can subtract 1 from the first addend and then compensate by adding 1 to the second addend. Addition is easy now because I can add 47 to 20 to get to 67. I can add any number to one addend as long as I subtract the same number I added from the second addend.

TIPS

- Number talks help students understand that numbers can be composed and decomposed to make new numbers.

- Make sure all students are participating and listening respectively.

- For students struggling with abstract thinking, go back to a number line.

QUESTIONS

- How is 48 + 19 similar to 47 + 20? How is it different? Is the sum the same or different?

- What is your estimated answer to this problem?

- How did we manipulate the numbers to make addition easier?

- How do you know which number to adjust?

- Does it matter which addend you add 1 to and which you subtract 1 from? Will the solution still be the same?

- What does this look like on a number line?

Compensation to Add: Number Talks

21 + 38	35 + 38	47 + 38
55 + 27	72 + 19	61 + 37
66 + 29	24 + 19	52 + 39
32 + 29	42 + 29	71 + 21
53 + 38	12 + 19	63 + 28
18 + 59	13 + 67	28 + 13
22 + 49	34 + 38	36 + 28
45 + 29	48 + 26	57 + 17

Compensation to Subtract

What is 58 − 39?

58 − 39

+1

----

58 − 40 = 18

18 + 1 = 19

I can mentally solve this subtraction problem by using compensation. I add 1 to the subtrahend, making it 40. Now it's easy to subtract 58 − 40 to get 18. Because I added 1 to the subtrahend, I need to add 1 to the difference. This way, the distance between the two numbers stays the same. 18 + 1 = 19.

TIPS

• This is the same strategy as equivalent expressions, just in a different format. It does not use the number line to show the distance remaining the same.

• If the student struggles with this abstract thought, use the number line and equivalent expressions.

• Start with smaller numbers and gradually add in more complex numbers for a second grade student.

QUESTIONS

• Will you compensate by adding or subtracting a set number?

• What does this look like on a number line?

• Would this work better on a hundreds chart?

• How many different strategies can you think of to solve this problem?

Compensation to Subtract: Number Talks

100 − 59	19 − 12	96 − 28
26 − 19	46 − 39	58 − 23
90 − 49	80 − 58	34 − 28
33 − 19	52 − 39	94 − 21
76 − 29	44 − 28	66 − 48
18 − 14	29 − 13	32 − 19
48 − 34	54 − 28	69 − 35
93 − 59	88 − 62	79 − 48

Adding Using Friendly Numbers to Look for Tens

What is 57 + 34?

3   31

(57 + 3) + 31

60 + 31 = 91

Using friendly numbers makes mental math easy. Since 57 is just 3 units away from 60, I decompose 34 into 3 + 31. Now, I can combine the 3 with 57 to make a nice friendly number, 60. Addition is easy now because 60 + 31 is 91.

TIPS

- Make sure to write down student responses and ask clarifying questions.
- Number talks are student driven. Teachers remain facilitators of the discussions.
- The purpose of a number talk is to empower students to be mathematically proficient.
- Students should be able to use an algorithm but also models and estimations. They should be able to explain their reasoning.
- Remind students what friendly numbers are and how they help with mental math.

QUESTIONS

- What is your estimated answer to this problem?
- How does decomposing a number help you add?

- Can you explain what a friendly number is? How do friendly numbers make addition easier?
- Could we have decomposed the other addend to make friendly numbers?
- Is there an easier strategy? Explain.

Adding Using Friendly Numbers to Look for Tens: Number Talks

16 + 28	38 + 27	27 + 38
48 + 25	35 + 36	47 + 24
29 + 42	41 + 39	18 + 54
17 + 68	37 + 26	28 + 53
55 + 26	66 + 17	58 + 23
13 + 49	17 + 38	25 + 48
23 + 39	37 + 48	49 + 17
52 + 18	69 + 24	62 + 29

Counting Back
Using Abstract Thought

What is 92 − 53?

| 92 | 82 | 72 | 62 | 52 | 42 | 41 | 40 | 39 |

I know that 53 is composed of 5 tens and 3 ones. I can subtract using abstract thought. I start with my minuend, 92, and I subtract 5 groups of 10, then 3 ones. My end number, 39, is the difference between 92 and 53.

TIPS

- For struggling students, show this using a number line. If necessary, use smaller numbers.
- Encourage students to think about mathematics in a way that makes sense to them.
- Number talks will help students be accurate, efficient, and flexible in their thinking and reasoning.
- Create a learning environment where all students feel they can share, discuss, and analyze their work and the work of others.

QUESTIONS

- What is your estimated answer for this problem?
- Why do you start with the minuend when counting back?
- Would your answer be the same if you started with the subtrahend?
- How do you know the number of groups of tens and ones to count back by?
- Does this strategy make subtraction easier?
- How can you explain your thinking to a friend?

Counting Back Using Abstract Thought: Number Talks

85 – 43	75 – 36	63 – 41
51 – 32	98 – 46	53 – 17
72 – 47	81 – 68	99 – 62
92 – 37	68 – 44	79 – 51
67 – 44	58 – 36	87 – 26
46 – 32	49 – 18	44 – 26
38 – 16	35 – 12	94 – 56
83 – 37	75 – 28	64 – 35

Partial Sums: Adding Left to Right

What is 47 + 25?

$$
\begin{array}{r}
47 \\
+\ 25 \\
\hline
60 \longleftarrow 40 + 20 \\
+\ 12 \longleftarrow 7 + 5 \\
\hline
72
\end{array}
$$

Instead of using the traditional method of addition, where I add right to left, I can add left to right using partial sums. First, I add the numbers in the tens place (40 + 20), then I add the numbers in the ones place (7 + 5). To get my final sum of 47 + 25, I add the partial sums: 60 + 12 = 72.

TIPS

- Listen carefully to student strategies before writing them down. You want to be accurate when you recount the strategies that have been shared.

- When you end a number talk, you should reflect on what a student has learned or will be learning during core instruction.

- Make sure the problem you select for a number talk can easily be solved using mental math.

- Focus your number talk on mental math computation.

QUESTIONS

- What is your estimate for the answer? Is your estimate close to the answer?

- How many different strategies can you think of to solve this problem?

- How are your strategies the same or different from those of your classmates?

- Can you get the correct answer if you add left to right instead of right to left? Prove your thinking.

- Can you explain this strategy in your own words?

- Is this strategy similar or different from another strategy you know?

Partial Sums: Adding Left to Right: Number Talks

12 + 15	22 + 35	42 + 19
48 + 35	55 + 24	47 + 29
42 + 26	18 + 21	26 + 31
14 + 16	53 + 27	38 + 52
63 + 24	42 + 37	61 + 28
35 + 27	32 + 29	37 + 15
58 + 24	65 + 18	25 + 46
24 + 38	13 + 67	33 + 54

"Adding To"

I know that 21 apples plus 12 more will make a total of 33 apples.

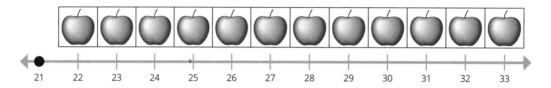

Parts
?
21 | 12

21 + 12 = ?

21 + ? = 33

? + 12 = 33

21 + 12 = 33

Change Unknown:

Eric picked 21 apples.
He then picked some more.
Now there are 33 apples.
How many did he pick?

21 + ? = 33

Result Unknown:

Eric picked 21 apples.
He then picked 12 more.
How many apples did he pick?

21 + 12 = ?

Start Unknown:

Eric picked some apples.
He then picked 12 more apples.
Now he has 33 apples?
How many did he originally pick?

? + 12 = 33

TIPS

• Use counters or other manipulatives so struggling learners can mirror the problem.

• Make sure students share their thinking with the class.

• Look for conceptual understanding and not just memorization of a mathematical procedure.

• Have students solve the problem mentally before asking for a strategy.

• Provide sufficient wait time.

"Adding To": Result Unknown

12 fish are in one bowl. 3 fish are in another bowl.

How many fish are there?

QUESTIONS

- What numbers are being added? Show a thumbs-up when you have a strategy and solution.
- How many fish are in the first tank?
- How many fish are in the second tank?
- How many total fish are in both tanks?
- What strategy did you use to find your solution? Describe your strategy.
- What addition number sentence models this picture?

- The number sentence says 12 and 3 more is 15. How does this picture show this?
- How would you describe this sentence using a number line?
- How would you show this number sentence using connecting cubes, ten-frames, or base ten blocks?
- How can you prove your answer using a part-part-whole model?

"Adding To": Change Unknown

5 animals are behind a fence. Some other animals join the first group behind the fence. Now there are 12 animals behind the fence. How many animals joined the group?

QUESTIONS

- How many total animals are there? Give a thumbs-up when you have a strategy and solution to the problem. Record student responses.

- How many animals are behind the fence?

- How many animals joined the group?

- What addition number sentence models this picture? What strategy did you use to find your number sentence?

- The number sentence says 5 and 7 more is 12. How does this picture show this?

- How would you describe this number sentence using a number line?

- How would you show this number sentence using connecting cubes, ten-frames, or base ten blocks?

- How can you prove your answer?

- Does everyone agree on the correct total and number sentence?

"Adding To":
Start Unknown

Laura's candy jar was packed with candy. She was able
to add 24 more pieces to the jar. Now there are 67 pieces of candy
in the jar. How many pieces of candy were in the jar to begin with?

QUESTIONS

- What is your estimated number of pieces of candy?

- How many pieces of candy do you think she started with?

- What strategy did you use to find your solution? Explain your strategy to your neighbor.

- What number sentence will help us solve this problem?

- What numbers are the parts and what number is the whole?

- How do you show your answer on an open number line?

- Describe the strategy you find the easiest to use.

- What number bond will match this problem?

- How do you know your answer is right? Explain using a model.

"Adding To": Number Talks

Mike put 14 pencils on the table. He added 23 pencils. How many pencils are there now?	There were 30 frogs in the pond. Then some more hopped in. Now there are 50 frogs. How many hopped in?	Steve caught some butterflies. He then caught 12 more. Now he has 44 butterflies. How many did he have to start with?
There are 36 color counters on the table. Kari added 32 color counters. How many color counters are now on the table?	Paul counted 51 stars in the sky. He then saw more stars. Now his count is up to 74 stars. How many more did he see?	There are apples in a basket. Then 34 more apples were added. There are now 86 apples in the basket. How many were in the basket to start with?
Sue read 16 pages. She then read 13 more. How many pages did she read?	There are 15 students in class. More students joined the class. Now the class has 26 students. How many more came in?	Some friends are in a pool. 12 more jumped in. Now there are 28 friends in the pool. How many were in the pool before more friends jumped in?
Sophie has 22 math problems for homework. Her mom added more for her to do. If she has to complete 35 problems, how many did her mom add?	Quinn counted 35 penguins in the zoo. The zoo keeper brought in 16 more. How many penguins are now in the zoo?	Carolyn watched several parrots in a tree. Then, 15 more flew into the tree. Now there are 40 parrots in the tree. How many were in the tree to start with?

"Taking From"

Tara caught 19 bugs in a net. 7 bugs flew away.
How many bugs are left in the net?

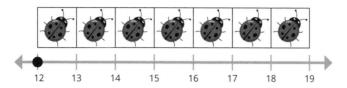

19	
7	?

19 − 7 = ?

19 − ? = 12

? − 7 = 12

19 − 7 = 12

Change Unknown:

Tara caught 19 bugs in a net. Some of the bugs flew away.
Then there were 12 bugs in the net. How many flew away?

19 − ? = 12

Result Unknown:

Tara caught 19 bugs in a net.
7 bugs flew away.
How many bugs are left in the net?

19 − 7 = ?

Start Unknown:

Tara caught many bugs in her net.
7 bugs flew away. Now she has 12 bugs left in the net. How many did she catch to begin with?

? − 7 = 12

TIPS

- A number talk should be a quick mental math practice.
- Record student thinking and ask questions to encourage mathematic discussions.
- Focus on the mathematical practices along with conceptual understanding.
- Keep in mind that a number talk goes well beyond memorizing a procedure.
- Enjoy number talks. They could be the best part of the student's day.

"Taking From": Result Unknown

10 cups sat on the table. 2 fell off the table.
How many remain on the table?

QUESTIONS

- Does 10 take away 2 have the same solution as 2 take away 10?

- Can you describe a subtraction number sentence using 10, 2, and 8?

- How are these two number sentences related?

- Is 8 = 10 − 2 the same as 10 − 2 = 8? How are they alike and how are they different? How do you know?

- How do you know this picture shows a subtraction problem?

- Is there another strategy you used to find your solution? Describe your strategy.

- What would happen if...?

- How do you know...?

"Taking From": Change Unknown

11 birds sat in a tree. Several birds flew away.
There were 5 birds left. How many flew away?

QUESTIONS

- Give me a thumbs-up if you have a strategy and solution.

- What is the solution to this problem?

- What is the unknown in the problem? What are the parts?

- How many birds flew away?

- Can you describe the strategy you used to solve this problem? Share with your neighbor.

- How can you show your answer using a number line?

- What number sentence will match this problem?

- How are the numbers 11, 6, and 5 related?

- Can you give me a subtraction number sentence that would prove your answer?

"Taking From":
Start Unknown

Some chocolates are in a jar. I ate 14 of the chocolates.
Then there were 9. How many were in the jar before some were eaten?

QUESTIONS

- Do you have an answer to this problem? Give me a thumbs-up if you have a strategy.

- What is the solution to this problem?

- What is the unknown in the problem?

- How many chocolates were there to begin with?

- What strategy did you use to solve this problem? Share with your neighbor.

- How can you show your answer using a number line?

- Can you give a number sentence to match this problem?

- What are the parts and what is the whole?

- How do you know your answer is right? Share with your neighbor.

- Can you give me a subtraction number sentence that would prove your answer?

"Taking From": Number Talks

There are 30 books on the shelf. I took 20. How many books are now on the shelf?	Mina baked 48 cupcakes. She gave some away. She now has 22 cupcakes. How many did she give away?	Some cherries were in a bowl. 40 cherries were used for pies. There are now 50 cherries left. How many cherries were in the bowl before the pies were made?
There are 64 horses in the pen. Bob removed 33. How many horses are now in the pen?	A pitcher holds 36 cups of juice. Several cups of juice were used. 12 cups of juice remain. How many cups of juice were used?	The school bus holds many kids. 12 kids got off the bus. Then there were 12 kids on the bus. How many were on the bus before some got off?
Ira's book has 55 pages. He read 23 of the pages. How many more are there to read?	A baseball card collection holds 49 cards. Kit gave away some cards. Now he has 14 cards. How many cards did he give away?	Mike has a box of crayons. He threw away 21 crayons. He now has 43 left. How many were in the box before he threw some away?
Lilly has 45 crayons in her box. She shared 26 crayons. How many are left in her box?	Laura has a box of marbles. She took out 18. Now she has 27 left. How many were in the box before she took some out?	A butterfly net holds 62 butterflies. Some of the butterflies flew away. Now there are 28 butterflies left in the net. How many butterflies flew away?

Put Together/Take Apart

Mina picked 6 yellow tulips and 8 red tulips.
How many tulips did she pick?

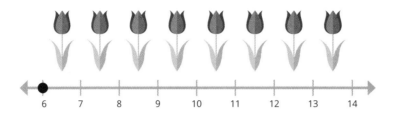

14	
6	8

$6 + 8 = 14$

$6 + ? = 14$

$? + 8 = 14$

Total Unknown:

Mina picked 6 yellow tulips and 8 red tulips. How many tulips did she pick?

$6 + 8 = ?$

One Addend Unknown:

Mina picked 14 tulips.
If she picked 6 yellow tulips, how many tulips were red?

$6 + ? = 14$

Both Addends Unknown:

Mina picked 14 tulips. How many could have been red and how many could have been yellow?

Examples of Possible Addends:

$14 + 0 = 14$	$12 + 2 = 14$
$0 + 14 = 14$	$7 + 7 = 14$
$1 + 13 = 14$	$5 + 9 = 14$
$2 + 12 = 14$	$9 + 5 = 14$

TIPS

- Number talks are usually done whole group. However, they can be done in small settings, at after-school tutoring, at home, in intervention classes, or individually.
- Number talks are a great way to look for and understand student errors.
- Differentiate your number talks with questioning and by providing different levels of difficulty.
- Short daily number talks are more powerful than long, drawn-out number talks. They should not replace core instruction.

Put Together/Take Apart: Total Unknown

There are 5 dark gray, 9 medium gray, and 10 light gray ladybugs in my garden.

How many ladybugs are in my garden?

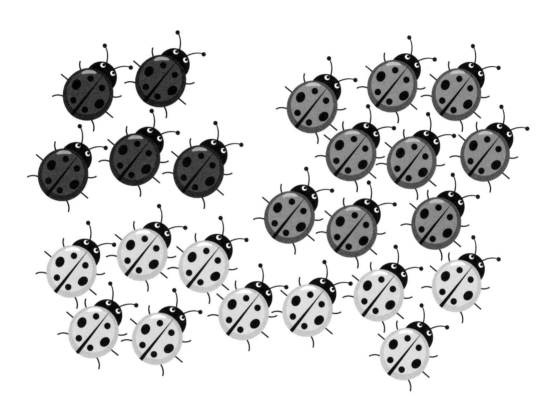

QUESTIONS

- What strategy did you use to get your answer?
- Can you explain your strategy?
- Do we all agree on the correct answer?
- How do you prove your answer is correct?
- Which strategy did you like best? Explain to a friend.

Put Together/Take Apart: One Addend Unknown

Twenty butterflies are on a bush. Thirteen are blue and the rest are orange. How many butterflies are orange?

QUESTIONS

- What is the problem asking us?
- How many total butterflies do we have?
- How many butterflies are blue?
- How many butterflies are orange?
- What number sentence will help us find the number of orange butterflies?
- What strategy will you use to find the number of orange butterflies?
- Can you explain your strategy?
- How can you check to see if your answer is correct?
- Can you explain your answer using a part-part-whole chart?
- What numbers are the parts and what is the whole?

Put Together/Take Apart: Both Addends Unknown

Mom has 13 apples. How many can she use for baking and how many can she save for eating?

QUESTIONS

- Who would like to share their solution to the problem?
- How many different number sentences can you describe?
- How did you get your answer?
- Are there any missing solutions?
- Does anyone have a different solution to the problem?
- Are there any other possible solutions?

Put Together/Take Apart: Number Talks

Peter has 14 white socks and 24 black socks. How many socks does he have?	22 students are in second grade. 15 are girls and the rest are boys. How many boys are there?	Candice has 10 chocolates. She wants to put some in a bowl and then eat the rest. How many can she put in a bowl and how many can she eat?
Mary scored 6 baskets and then another 10 baskets in basketball. How many baskets did she score?	Laura has 15 books. There are 9 chapter books and the rest are picture books. How many picture books are there?	Steve has 8 fish. He can either freeze them or eat them. How many can he freeze and how many can he eat?
There are 13 green pencils and 12 blue pencils on the teacher's desk. How many pencils are on the desk?	There are 16 movies showing at the theater. 4 of the movies are children's movies and the rest are dramas. How many movies are dramas?	9 children are going to the movies. Some are going to see the new Star Wars movie and some are seeing the latest Disney movie. How many can go to each different movie?
There are 14 boys and 16 girls in second grade. How many children are in second grade?	George downloaded 12 songs from his mom's phone. He can save them or delete them. If he saved 5 songs, how many will he delete?	Claire has 36 cousins. Fourteen live in her hometown and the rest out of state. How many cousins live out of state?

Comparison Problems

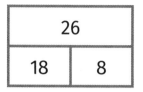

Shelley has 18 cookies. Jim has 26 cookies.
How many more cookies does Jim have than Shelley?

26	
18	8

Shelly	18	?
Jim	26	

18 + ? = 26

26 − 18 = ?

Jim has 8 more cookies than Shelley OR Shelley has 8 fewer cookies than Jim.

TIPS

- Asking students to discuss and analyze their strategies out loud helps solidify their thinking.
- Asking for a thumbs-up instead of a hand in the air allows the teacher to see who can compute mentally and who is struggling with the computation.
- Always start with small numbers so everyone has an opportunity to be successful. Build on successes.

QUESTIONS

- What is the problem asking?
- How do you know what strategy to use?
- How do you know whether to add or subtract?
- What number sentence will help you solve the problem?
- What are we comparing?

- Can someone explain that strategy in their own words?
- Did you understand that strategy? Can you restate it? How does it work?
- Can you prove your answer?
- Does using a tape diagram help you visualize this problem?

Comparison Problems: Number Talks

Rich scored 13 points. Nancy scored 7 points. How many fewer points did Nancy score than Rich?	Larry made 8 more cupcakes than Jenny. Jenny made 10 cupcakes. How many cupcakes did Larry make?	Laura caught 6 more fish than Mike. Laura caught 15 fish. How many fish did Mike catch?
I have 16 colored pencils. My friend has 11 colored pencils. How many more pencils do I have than my friend?	Bob has 5 fewer math problems than Joyce. Bob has 20 math problems. How many math problems does Joyce have?	Linda has 10 fewer crayons than Ron. Linda has 20 crayons. How many crayons does Ron have?
Sara has 8 more pages to read than Bob has. Sara read 20 pages. How many pages did Bob read?	Cathy made 18 baskets. Steve made 8 baskets. How many fewer baskets did Steve make than Cathy?	Andy has 20 more minutes of homework than Julie. Julie has 12 minutes of homework. How many minutes of homework does Andy have?
Jerry has 15 fewer cupcakes than Rose. Jerry has 45 cupcakes. How many cupcakes does Rose have?	Jenny has 32 fewer cousins than Larry. Jenny has 64 cousins. How many cousins does Larry have?	Mary found 23 ladybugs. Elwyn found 31 ladybugs. How many more ladybugs did Elwyn find than Mary?

Appendix

Common Addition and Subtraction[1]

	Result Unknown	Change Unknown	Start Unknown
Add To	Two bunnies sat on the grass. Three more bunnies hopped there. How many bunnies are on the grass now? **2 + 3 = ?**	Two bunnies were sitting on the grass. Some more bunnies hopped there. Then there were five bunnies. How many bunnies hopped over to the first two? **2 + ? = 5**	Some bunnies were sitting on the grass. Three more bunnies hopped there. Then there were five bunnies. How many bunnies were on the grass before? **? + 3 = 5**
Take From	Five apples were on the table. I ate two apples. How many apples are on the table now? **5 – 2 = ?**	Five apples were on the table. I ate some apples. Then there were three apples. How many apples did I eat? **5 – ? = 3**	Some apples were on the table. I ate two apples. Then there were three apples. How many apples were on the table before? **? – 2 = 3**
	Total Unknown	**Addend Unknown**	**Both Addends Unknown[2]**
Put Together/ Take Apart[3]	Three red apples and two green apples are on the table. How many apples are on the table? **3 + 2 = ?**	Five apples are on the table. Three are red and the rest are green. How many apples are green? **3 + ? = 5, 5 – 3 = ?**	Grandma has five flowers. How many can she put in the red vase and how many in her blue vase? **5 = 0 + 5, 5 = 1 + 4, 5 = 2 + 3**
	Difference Unknown	**Bigger Unknown**	**Smaller Unknown**
	How many more?: Lucy has two apples. Julie has five apples. How many more apples does Julie have than Lucy? **2 + ? = 5** How many fewer?: Lucy has two apples. Julie has five apples. How many fewer apples does Lucy have than Julie? **5 – 2 = ?**	More: Julie has three more apples than Lucy. Lucy has two apples. How many apples does Julie have? **2 + 3 = ?** Fewer: Lucy has 3 fewer apples than Julie. Lucy has two apples. How many apples does Julie have? **3 + 2 = ?**	More: Julie has three more apples than Lucy. Julie has five apples. How many apples does Lucy have? **5 – 3 = ?** Fewer: Lucy has 3 fewer apples than Julie. Julie has five apples. How many apples does Lucy have? **? + 3 = 5**

1 Adapted from Box 2-4 of Mathematics Learning in Early Childhood, National Research Council (2009, pp. 32, 33).

2 These take apart situations can be used to show all the decompositions of a given number. The associated equations, which have the total on the left of the equal sign, help children understand that the = sign does not always mean, makes or results in but always does mean is the same number as.

3 Either addend can be unknown, so there are three variations of these problem situations. Both addends Unknown is a productive extension of the basic situation, especially for small numbers less than or equal to 10.

Artwork Credits

All images from Shutterstock.com

page 8: kids table © canbedone

page 10: girl at chalkboard
  © Vladgrin

page 12: pumpkins © suesse

page 13: dogs © KittyVector

page 13: fish © Jibon

page 13: heart © Maxim Matsevich

page 14: markers © casejustin

page 13: mice © Maquiladora

page 14: skateboarders © Iconic
  Bestiary

page 14: umbrellas © M.Stasy

page 20: boy © brgfx

page 24: castle and bridge
  © Alfmaler

page 24 :dragons © Vectors Bang

page 25: fish tank © kontur-vid

page 26: pool party © brgfx

page 27: animals on bus © Sujono
  sujono

page 29: climbing © brgfx

page 30: animals on train
  © nataka

page 31: apple tree © stockakia

page 32: birds © GraphicsRF

page 33: butterflies © MicroOne

page 34: construction © Andrii
  Bezvershenko

page 35: owls © Julianka

page 36: animals on bus
  © hermandesign2015

page 36: bees
  © hermandesign2015

page 36: cups © Elvetica

page 37: bugs © keyplacement

page 37: kids table © canbedone

page 37: pies © Sandra Jones
  Illustration

page 38: apple picking © Lanaart

page 38: family © Olga1818

page 38: sandwich © Michele
  Paccione

page 39: catepillars
  © BlueRingMedia

page 39: kites © graphic-line

page 39: zebra train © nataka

page 43: train © Tatiana Shepeleva

pages 44–47: train © nataka

pages 47–49: frogs © Maquiladora

page 50: butterflies © ecco

page 51: blocks © sonia

page 51: flowers © daisybee

page 51: dragons © Vectors Bang

page 51: ice cream © Shirstok

page 52: cars © Mascha Tace

page 52: fish © fredrisher

page 52: peanut butter and jelly
  © Cute Designs

page 53: book © Oxy_gen

page 53: birds © tn-prints

page 53: calculator © Dmitry
  Guzhanin

page 53: kites © M.Stasy

page 54: football helmet
  © moenez

page 54: hands © Fedorov Oleksiy

page 54: scales © VectorKnight

page 58: birds © tn-prints

page 59: abacus © BlueRingMedia

page 59: globe © Sabelskaya

page 59: worm © Palugada

page 59: dogs © KittyVector

page 59: mouse © Maquiladora

page 60: turtles © ONYXprj

page 60: zebra © Biscotto87

page 61: glue stick © Dzm1try

page 61: pencil © Kolesov Sergei

page 61: scissors © Ain Mikail

page 65: kids chalkboard © brgfx

page 84: turtles © ONYXprj

page 85: mountain climbing
  © brgfx

page 86: family © Isarapic

page 88: animal bus
  © hermandesign2015

page 112: boy at chalkboard © Krol

page 114: girl at chalkboard © brgfx

page 127: children © FoxyImage

page 191: fish bowls © Tomacco

page 192: animals © nataka

page 193: candy jar © Lorelyn
  Medina

page 195: ladybug © Spreadthesign

page 196: cups © Elvetica

page 197: tree © Guz Anna

page 198: candy jar © Lomingo

page 200: tulips © Aliaksei_7799

page 201: ladybugs
  © Spreadthesign

page 202: butterflies © ecco

page 205: cookies
  © BlueRingMedia

About the Author

Nancy Hughes, author of *Classroom-Ready Number Talks for 3rd, 4th and 5th Grade Teachers*, spent the last 10 years as K–12 mathematics coordinator at Olathe Public Schools, the largest school district in the Kansas City region, where she also provided professional development for mathematics teachers in all grade levels. Prior to working in Olathe, Hughes taught middle school math in Kansas City area public and private schools. Hughes has presented math topics at conferences for the National Council of Teachers of Mathematics, Kansas City Area Teachers of Mathematics, and Kansas Area Teachers of Mathematics. She also directed the Kauffman Foundation's K–16 Professional Development program. Hughes has a B.S. from Kansas State University and an M.S. in Curriculum and Instruction from Kansas University.